SpringerBriefs in Education

We are delighted to announce SpringerBriefs in Education, an innovative product type that combines elements of both journals and books. Briefs present concise summaries of cutting-edge research and practical applications in education. Featuring compact volumes of 50 to 125 pages, the SpringerBriefs in Education allow authors to present their ideas and readers to absorb them with a minimal time investment. Briefs are published as part of Springer's eBook Collection. In addition, Briefs are available for individual print and electronic purchase.

SpringerBriefs in Education cover a broad range of educational fields such as: Science Education, Higher Education, Educational Psychology, Assessment & Evaluation, Language Education, Mathematics Education, Educational Technology, Medical Education and Educational Policy.

SpringerBriefs typically offer an outlet for:

- An introduction to a (sub)field in education summarizing and giving an overview of theories, issues, core concepts and/or key literature in a particular field
- A timely report of state-of-the art analytical techniques and instruments in the field of educational research
- A presentation of core educational concepts
- An overview of a testing and evaluation method
- A snapshot of a hot or emerging topic or policy change
- An in-depth case study
- A literature review
- A report/review study of a survey
- An elaborated thesis

Both solicited and unsolicited manuscripts are considered for publication in the SpringerBriefs in Education series. Potential authors are warmly invited to complete and submit the Briefs Author Proposal form. All projects will be submitted to editorial review by editorial advisors.

SpringerBriefs are characterized by expedited production schedules with the aim for publication 8 to 12 weeks after acceptance and fast, global electronic dissemination through our online platform SpringerLink. The standard concise author contracts guarantee that:

- an individual ISBN is assigned to each manuscript
- each manuscript is copyrighted in the name of the author
- the author retains the right to post the pre-publication version on his/her website or that of his/her institution

John Willison
Editor

Research Thinking for Responsive Teaching

Research Skill Development with In-service and Preservice Educators

Springer

Editor
John Willison
School of Education
University of Adelaide
Adelaide, SA, Australia

ISSN 2211-1921　　　　　　　ISSN 2211-193X　(electronic)
SpringerBriefs in Education
ISBN 978-981-99-6678-3　　　ISBN 978-981-99-6679-0　(eBook)
https://doi.org/10.1007/978-981-99-6679-0

© The Editor(s) (if applicable) and The Author(s) 2024. This book is an open access publication.

Open Access This book is licensed under the terms of the Creative Commons Attribution 4.0 International License (http://creativecommons.org/licenses/by/4.0/), which permits use, sharing, adaptation, distribution and reproduction in any medium or format, as long as you give appropriate credit to the original author(s) and the source, provide a link to the Creative Commons license and indicate if changes were made.
The images or other third party material in this book are included in the book's Creative Commons license, unless indicated otherwise in a credit line to the material. If material is not included in the book's Creative Commons license and your intended use is not permitted by statutory regulation or exceeds the permitted use, you will need to obtain permission directly from the copyright holder.
The use of general descriptive names, registered names, trademarks, service marks, etc. in this publication does not imply, even in the absence of a specific statement, that such names are exempt from the relevant protective laws and regulations and therefore free for general use.
The publisher, the authors, and the editors are safe to assume that the advice and information in this book are believed to be true and accurate at the date of publication. Neither the publisher nor the authors or the editors give a warranty, expressed or implied, with respect to the material contained herein or for any errors or omissions that may have been made. The publisher remains neutral with regard to jurisdictional claims in published maps and institutional affiliations.

This Springer imprint is published by the registered company Springer Nature Singapore Pte Ltd.
The registered company address is: 152 Beach Road, #21-01/04 Gateway East, Singapore 189721, Singapore

Paper in this product is recyclable.

Preface

The proliferation of readily available artificial intelligence is the next installment in a series of factors that have caused educators to inhale sharply and think about their responses in order to enhance student learning. Responsive teaching is the drive to improve the learning of those under one's care and is based on recognizing and consolidating what is useful as well as the resourcefulness and adaptability to enhance, add, or change. This book aims to enable teachers to be responsive to student needs and context demands, and so be increasingly autonomous professionals. Education 4.0 in the Fourth Industrial Revolution requires teachers who are or becoming ICT savvy regardless of country or context. But being armed with a plethora of associated digital tools and emerging pedagogies is not adequate; it is teachers' sense of purpose and strong conceptualization of student learning and their own practice that underpin teacher professional autonomy and responsiveness.

The conceptualization of this book concerns teachers' research thinking that promotes this responsive teaching. The eight chapters of this book share the Research Skill Development framework as a conceptualization that guides teacher research thinking, adapted, and expressed in ways that fit the diverse contexts across the chapters. Contexts include classroom teachers in geographically remote high schools or engaging in further study, in Australia and Canada; preservice teachers engaged in digitally enabled learning in Indonesia and Australia, or course-based undergraduate research in the USA; and university educators embracing communities of practice as part of Educational Development programs in Canada and the USA.

This book is therefore for teacher educators and school teachers, whether already registered and working in the classroom or preservice teachers engaged in Initial Teacher Education programs, as well as those who run Educational Development programs for university teachers. The book's Chap. 1 introduces the Research Skill Development (RSD) framework, providing the conceptual framing for each subsequent chapter, and articulates the need for, and characteristics of, teacher research thinking. Part I pertains to practicing teacher research thinking, with Chap. 2 set in a secondary school classroom context, Chaps. 3 and 4 are about classroom teachers who are engaged in further study, and Chap. 5 is on the Educational Development of university educators. Part II provides three chapters on initial teacher education, with Chaps. 6 and 7 focusing on preservice teacher digital skills and Chap. 8 on course-based undergraduate research experiences.

There are pressures that trivialize teacher professionalism, reducing it perhaps to a technical response that implements others' research. This book provides a diverse range of ways of enhancing teacher professional practice, not by reducing it to a technical, assured enterprise but by expansive thinking. Expansive and responsive thinking is that which teachers need and use when dealing with the realities of their students in the diverse and changing landscapers that comprise education across the four countries represented.

Adelaide, Australia John Willison
December 2023

Acknowledgments The authors of this book are grateful to the reviews provided by the following colleagues.

Lucia Ravi, University of Western Australia
Lyn Torres, Monash University
Ros Woodhouse, York University, Canada
Walter Barbieri, Kristy Davis, Lynda McCleod, Parivash Nezhad, Fizza Sabir, and Linda Westphalen, University of Adelaide.

Contents

1 **Teachers' Research Thinking** 1
   John Willison

Part I In-service Teachers' Research Thinking

2 **High School Student Experiences of Teacher Research Thinking** 17
   Jason Home, Tom Snelling, and John Willison

3 **Open Educational Practices (OEPs) for Research Skill Development with In-Service School Teachers** 33
   Barbara Brown, Michele Jacobsen, Verena Roberts,
   Christie Hurrell, Mia Travers, and Nicole Neutzling

4 **Exploring In-Service Teacher-Researcher Reflexivity: Education Research as Cultural Work** 49
   Deborah Heck

5 **Research-Oriented University Instruction: The Research Skill Development Framework and Communities of Practice** 65
   Sylvia Tiala and Kara Loy

Part II Preservice Teachers' Research Thinking

6 **Preservice Teachers' Use of Social Media for the Development of Their Research Skills** 85
   Raissa Mataniari, Asni Johari, Muhammad Rusdi,
   Bambang Hariyadi, and Finn Kristen Matthiesen

7 **Digital Skill Mythology and Understanding in Preservice Teachers** 105
   Amber McLeod

8 **Undergraduate Research for Preservice Teachers: Navigating Its Rich Complexity and Novel Possibilities** 121
Ruth J. Palmer

Glossary of Terms 139

Editor and Contributors

About the Editor

Dr. John Willison is the Director of the Bachelor of Teaching at the University of Adelaide and a National Senior Teaching Fellow. He was a secondary school science teacher for 10 years using systematic approaches to improving his students' learning. He has researched how teachers develop their students' research skills and other forms of sophisticated thinking for three decades.

Contributors

Barbara Brown The University of Calgary, Calgary, Canada

Bambang Hariyadi Universitas Jambi, Jambi, Indonesia

Deborah Heck University of the Sunshine Coast, Sippy Downs, Australia

Jason Home Victor Harbor High School, Victor Harbor, Australia

Christie Hurrell The University of Calgary, Calgary, Canada

Michele Jacobsen The University of Calgary, Calgary, Canada

Asni Johari Universitas Jambi, Jambi, Indonesia

Kara Loy Coast Mountain College, Terrace, Canada

Raissa Mataniari Universitas Jambi, Jambi, Indonesia

Finn Kristen Matthiesen University of Göttingen, Göttingen, Germany

Amber McLeod Monash University, Melbourne, Australia

Nicole Neutzling The University of Calgary, Calgary, Canada

Ruth J. Palmer The College of New Jersey, Ewing Township, USA

Verena Roberts The University of Calgary, Calgary, Canada

Muhammad Rusdi Universitas Jambi, Jambi, Indonesia

Tom Snelling Mercedes College, Adelaide, Australia

Sylvia Tiala University of Wisconsin–Stout, Menomonie, USA

Mia Travers The University of Calgary, Calgary, Canada

John Willison University of Adelaide, Adelaide, Australia

Abbreviations

CURE	Curriculum-based undergraduate research
ED	Educational Development
I-ST	In-service teacher
ITE	Initial teacher education
MELT	Models of Engaged Learning and Teaching
PST	Preservice teacher
RSD	Research Skill Development
TE	Teacher educator
UE	University educator
UGR	Undergraduate research

List of Figures

Fig. 3.1	Major assignments in four courses with alignment to RSD	36
Fig. 5.1	University educator's professional development ties to preservice and in-service teachers involved in pre-K to 12 education systems	67
Fig. 5.2	Average UE RSD—related professional development participation by student impact	73
Fig. 5.3	University educators' comfort levels teaching, assessing and integrating the RSD framework	73
Fig. 5.4	Evidence of university educator growth by professional development category	76
Fig. 6.1	Plant Taxonomy activities with the RSD facets involved	90
Fig. 6.2	A summary of PSTs' plant taxonomy Instagram post performance according to the RSD rubric level for each RSD facet	96
Fig. 8.1	Nested contexts of course integrated research experiences	125

List of Tables

Table 1.1	RSD facets, key questions and research thinking	4
Table 4.1	RSD embedded in course learning outcomes	51
Table 6.1	RSD rubric as the guidelines for PSTs in creating Instagram posts	91
Table 6.2	PST self-perception questionnaire responses	94
Table 7.1	Teacher analysis of vignette assessment using DSD framework	112
Table 7.2	Outline of Week 1–4 content and DSD framework focus	113
Table 7.3	Results of the pre- and post-survey of digital skills	116
Table 8.1	Cross table: design elements by instruction, course content & embedded research experience	127
Table 8.2	Research action, research thinking & RSD framework	131

Chapter 1
Teachers' Research Thinking

John Willison

Abstract In a world of unpredictable change, we need preservice and in-service school teachers, and university educators who can respond dynamically to students' diverse needs and the evolving demands on their lives. In this book, *research thinking* is used as an umbrella term for the raft of skills associated with such responsive teaching. Research thinking is needed so that teachers are both able to react quickly to contingencies and systematically adapt their practice through consolidation and change. The chapters of this book show how responsive research thinking in its various guises can help Preservice Teachers, In-Service Teachers, and University Educators to consolidate, change and connect through each chapter's use of the Research Skill Development (RSD) conceptual framework. This chapter outlines the need for teachers' research thinking, the nature of the RSD framework and what research thinking looks like with reference to the framework. This chapter then overviews how each chapter contributes to the book's theme of research thinking for responsive teaching before concluding with implications of the book for educational theory and practice.

1.1 Introduction

Research thinking is the term used in this book to communicate the idea of teachers engaging as mindful agents who discerningly adapt others' approaches based on research evidence as well as approaches to generate data and synthesise meaning in their own classrooms. Engaging with or consuming peer-reviewed and grey literature (such as in practice-oriented journals) requires sophisticated evaluation, translation and adaptation of concepts to each teaching context. Producing knowledge by thinking through and engaging in action research on their own classes is fundamental to teacher generation of contextually-situated information and data that enables decisions that influence student learning. This dual role as consumers and producers of research enables teachers to learn to make decisions about how to adapt to emerging

J. Willison (✉)
University of Adelaide, Adelaide, Australia
e-mail: john.willison@adelaide.edu.au

issues, sometimes responding quickly, sometimes planning proactively, and conveys this book's meaning of 'responsive teaching'. Teachers who are responsive sometimes take the time to identify and consolidate good practice, and at other times move quickly to adjust and change. Whenever consolidating or changing, responsive teachers endeavour to connect the components of learning in ways that students can join the dots.

This chapter focuses on the need for and nature of research thinking for Preservice Teachers (PSTs), In-service Teachers (I-STs) and University Educators (UEs), informed by the Research Skill Development (RSD) framework (Willison, 2018; Willison & O'Regan, 2007). Research thinking helps individual teachers consolidate good teaching practice, identify what may need to change and, crucially, make connections with colleagues. The chapter's perspective is that the shared framework and language of 'research thinking' facilitates connections with colleagues, theories and practices—within and across institutions—to improve student learning. Therefore, after introducing the RSD below and then defining research thinking with reference to it, this chapter overviews each of the other chapters, all of which use the RSD for the conceptual framing of research thinking. This overview helps to show the clear connections from PST education to I-ST education and educational development for UEs.

Research thinking embraces the cognitive, affective and relational aspects of thinking associated with the everyday interactions of the classroom as well as more systematic study, to solve problems that perplex and challenge teachers (Dewey, 1910). 'Research thinking…helps the teacher to see a problem systemically, solve the problems of non-standard character and high level of complexity.' (Rinatovna, 2017, p. 1411). Teacher research thinking is required and studied in teacher action research (McNiff, 1995), participatory action research (Kemmis, 2009), action learning (Zuber-Skerritt, 2002), evidence-based decision making (Willison et al., 2020), research-based teaching (Willcoxson et al., 2011) and the scholarship of teaching and learning (Cranton, 2011). Research thinking can also be modelled and facilitated by teachers, and so developed and used by students in problem-based learning, project-based learning, research-based learning, inquiry learning, collaborative learning, discovery learning and, frequently, in learning environments that blend face-to-face and online learning (Willison, 2020b). As an example, Chap. 2 of this book focuses on teacher research thinking, teacher real-time responses and their influence on secondary school student research skills.

This book's focus on responsive teaching has become, if possible, even more essential than it was four years ago. In addition to the usual and heavy demands on their adaptability, teachers worldwide have been responding to fast changes due to the complexities caused by COVID 19 and more recently by the easy access for students and teachers of Artificial Intelligence (see McLeod, Chap. 7 of this book). The changes demanded by COVID-19 and the acceleration of Artificial Intelligence use in educational contexts demonstrates that, at times, thoughtful responses enabled by research thinking of teachers, schools and universities are needed well before peer-reviewed research is conducted, let alone research-informed policy is formulated.

This book's focus on teacher research thinking, then, is timely because it highlights and provides a range of ways to facilitate the development of responsive teaching. Responsiveness may be needed because of sudden contingencies, because of day-to-day factors or slower evolution of circumstances. One of these evolving circumstances is that, increasingly the '…codification of knowledge or practice is privileged over the professional judgement of teachers' (Hallman et al., 2022, p. 127). Codified knowledge and practice are stripped of contextual understanding, imply rigidity over responsiveness and reduces the salience of teacher professional judgement. Furthermore, less responsive classroom practice and reduced teacher professionalism may have the opposite effect of the intended educational aims of codified practice. In our era of unpredictable change, maximising educator capacity for professional judgement and response to emerging needs is vital (De Vos et al., 2019). This is because improvement in teaching involves an ongoing quest to enhance student learning, including the identification and consolidation of existing helpful practice as well as new practice, rather than codification of practice: 'Codification is a dangerous thing when change is inevitable.' (Hallman et al., 2022, p. 127). Through teacher responsiveness throughout COVID-19 and AI's emergence as a major educational factor, perhaps more than ever education systems should be able to appreciate the need for teacher responsiveness over codification of practice.

Research thinking in this book is seen as a term that prioritises teacher professional judgement which heeds, but is not diffident with respect to, others' research. This book's vision of research thinking emphasises a balance between others' published evidence and a teacher's own evidence from practice. Mentalities around educational research seem to emphasize, on one hand a reliance on pre-specified curriculum and pedagogical approaches developed and validated through others' research or, on the other hand, teacher-research (Willison et al., 2020). We may ask of those who state that teaching must be based on evidence-based practice '*whose* evidence?'.

1.2 Research Thinking is Multifaceted

The RSD is the overarching conceptual framework for this book. The authors of Chaps. 2–8 have adapted and implemented the RSD in their practice, and then researched their practice. In the decade following the first publication outlining the RSD (Willison & O'Regan, 2007), the framework was piloted and evaluated (Willison, 2012, 2018; Willison & Buisman-Pijlman, 2016; Willison et al., 2017, 2020; Wilmore & Willison, 2016), and critiqued (e.g., Brew, 2013; Spronken-Smith et al., 2013), revitalising the framework (see Willison, 2018 for a summary of changes in response to others' critique). There was an overarching sense that the framework addressed core elements of the sophisticated thinking that students and teachers needed to engage with and in, including in teacher education (Brew & Saunders, 2020).

In the RSD, the skills associated with research are articulated in six facets, each including verbs that make the research processes explicit, an integral affective dimension (Willison et al., 2020) and key question that each facet addresses (see Willison, 2018 for detailed descriptions of each facet). Table 1.1 shows how the facets correspond to the different forms of research thinking in which responsive educators engage.

Purposive thinking is developed and required as teachers work out what they are doing through an iterative process of embarking and clarifying, re-embarking and reclarifying. *Embark and clarify* are intentionally general verbs, chosen to convey the myriad ways that students and teachers work out what it is that they do, achieve, make or think about. This facet includes posing research questions or hypothesising, framing project goals, determining the parameters of a problem or issue, being piqued by a classroom occurrence or a conversation in the staffroom, or resolving to learn something. Repeated and diverse engagement in embarking develops, over time, *purposive thinking*. For educators, this may take the form of anything from literature reviews, theory testing in the classroom, to quick responses to classroom or school events, and leads to crisp and clear problem definition or redefined learning intentions for a lesson. A contention of this book is that all research thinking, including purposive thinking, is best developed in numerous diverse contexts over years (Moser et al., 2017) where teachers or students embark and clarify in many different ways. Thinking that develops a sense of purpose, direction and clarity is both an enabler and outcome of embarking on research, therefore the facet is epitomised by the question 'what is our purpose?' In affective terms, a major driver and outcome of research thinking is that the learning environment would enable the development of *curious* and *empathetic* teachers (Willison et al., 2020). The affective adjectives are indicative only: they are intended to inspire educator thought about what, in affective terms, they are striving to facilitate. It is the juxtaposition of verbs, affective adjective, key question and research thinking that represents the fulness of each facet and that describes research thinking.

Informed thinking is developed and used when teachers, in numerous contexts and with new perspectives, find information and generate data and ideas. *Find and generate* are verbs that drive teachers towards fresh perspectives, and so learn to use

Table 1.1 RSD facets, key questions and research thinking

Facet verbs	Facet affect	Key question	Research thinking
Embark and clarify	Curious/empathetic	What is our purpose?	*Purposive thinking*
Find and generate	Determined	What will we use?	*Informed thinking*
Evaluate and reflect	Discerning	What do we trust?	*Astute thinking*
Organise and manage	Harmonising	How do we arrange?	*Harmonising thinking*
Analyse and synthesise	Creative	What does it mean?	*Insightful thinking*
Communicate and apply	Constructive	How can we relate?	*Externalised thinking*

Adapted from the RSD in Willison (2018)

appropriate methodologies. Methodologies and outcomes of finding and generating often are viewed as 'research', however, in this book they comprise one facet of multi-faceted research thinking. The 're' in research imbues not merely more, but improved, refined and multi-faceted, thinking processes. Asking repeatedly 'what will we use?', *informed thinking* finds relevant information and, when this is insufficient, generates data as fuel for the research thinking. For teachers, treating the classroom as a perpetual site of real-time observation data is a substantial part of *informed thinking* and this enables real-time response, a powerful influence on student learning (Chin, 2006). Real-time response by teachers is, or can be, much more than a knee-jerk reaction if it is tuned and directed by multi-faceted research thinking.

*Astute thinking i*s facilitated by iteration after iteration of evaluation and reflection. *Evaluate and reflect* are processes where teachers determine the credibility of sources, information, data and ideas, and make their own research processes visible. The key question is 'what do we trust?' and the disposition wherein teachers become increasingly discerning. They determine the relevance and credibility of sources, information, data and ideas, curriculum documents and reviews and make their own research processes visible to themselves through reflection. Teachers look for stated and unstated biases in others' and their own educational information and data, and with each evaluation and reflection develop *astute thinking*. Astute thinking is not incredulous by default, but weighs up trustworthiness of parts and of the whole. Astute thinking applies this evaluative work to others' research and reflects on the effectiveness of one's own processes, including processes to review curriculum documents and research literature and to engage in classroom action research.

Harmonising thinking is progressively developed as teachers and students organise information and data to reveal patterns or themes, and manage teams, resources and processes. For example, Home (2017) used the RSD to develop a mind-map for a unit plan. The conceptual framework allowed him to clearly see and organise the learning emphases for the unit. To a large extent, analytical insight cannot be effectively generated unless organisational structures enable theme and pattern recognition, and so bringing information and data into harmony with issues being addressed is a major aspect of research thinking. Likewise, the harmonious arrangement of resources, teams and timeframes is a feature that enables other forms of research thinking. The central question for this facet, then, is 'how do we arrange?' Often organisation and management are seen to be merely technical, under-taught, under-developed and under-assessed (Willison, 2020a, 2020b). However, the enabling aspect of *harmonising thinking* means that teachers and students who do not develop this kind of thinking will struggle with all research thinking.

Insightful thinking is developed and employed as teachers and students learn time and again to analyse and synthesise. When teachers analyse information or data critically and synthesise new knowledge to produce coherent understandings, they are addressing the question 'what does it mean?' for classroom practice. Synthesis in particular has a creative element, where it is not just putting all the pieces together, but how they are so pieced. High school teachers are more likely than primary school teachers to focus on a limited range of subjects and have more specific conceptualisations about analysing and synthesising. It is crucial that all teachers form a fulsome understanding of these processes, because their analysis and synthesis are the keys to unlocking their own deepened understanding of the classroom, whether through 'eureka' insights or, more commonly, a slow-dawning process. If teachers have a technical-orientation to analysis and synthesis, this may disguise the variety of analytical thinking processes and rich synthesis of understanding enabled by insightful thinking that is broad and versatile. Such a technical orientation may prioritise quantitative analysis and the search for trends, or qualitative analysis and identification of themes, however it is the variety of analytical and synthesising perspectives that give rise to deeper insights into the classroom.

Without insightful thinking, teachers risk a narrow, technical perspective that can unwittingly disconnect student learning across subjects. There is every advantage for students to learn specific details and ways of analysing, for example identifying statistically significant trends in quantitative data in mathematics or economics or processes to identify themes in qualitative data in history or English. But students should simultaneously learn that different subject interpretations are all valid and useful ways of thinking analytically, that is, teachers should help students make connections between different forms of analysis and synthesis, so that students too learn to be insightful thinkers. The metacognitive *transfer* of thinking, such as analytical thinking, is notoriously difficult to facilitate or achieve (Scherpereel et al., 2022). For teachers to recognise, articulate and validate to students the different analytical and synthesising processes used by other teachers is a way to help students make connections, compound their learning and develop insightful thinking that is, or becomes, transferable.

Externalised thinking is developed through communication and application processes that are pushed out and pushed in. *Communicating* is a process of external expression when teachers discuss, listen, write, perform, respond to feedback and present processes, knowledge and implications of teaching. When teachers *apply* their understanding, heeding ethical, cultural, social and team issues and audience needs, they are expressing this understanding externally. *Pushed out* means that thinking starts internally and works its way to expression. For example, teachers may have an idea, a question, an insight and throw it out there verbally, pictorially, numerically, in text and/or with body language for other teachers or students to discuss or use. Pushed out also means taking an internalised educational concepts and applying them to a student, an online class or in professional development. *Pushed in* means that as teachers chat, discuss educational concepts or observe the application of concepts, these external stimuli, in concert with prior knowledge and experience, formulate an individual teacher's thinking. Whether starting or ending outside, externalised thinking is manifest.

If any facet of research thinking is missing, this reduces the capacity of that thinking to answer, solve or address issues or concerns of the school, classroom or students. If multi-faceted research thinking is explicit in teachers' minds, such as through the use of the RSD, it is more likely they will make explicit the nature of research thinking to school students, and examples of this are evident in Chap. 2.

In the RSD the six facets are elaborated along a continuum of learning autonomy (Willison & O'Regan, 2007. See Willison, 2018 for an updated version) which describes and guides, but does not prescribe, development of research thinking. Rather the RSD 'suggests that the learning environments needed for a promising future are ones in which every point provides value on the learning autonomy continuum.' (Fryer, 2022, p. 152). In the RSD autonomy is a 'tidal' concept, where movement back and forth is valued more than high or low levels in themselves, because this sense of movement can guide development that is relevant to the PST or the I-ST (see Willison et al., 2017 for a detailed description of autonomy and Chap. 7 for application). The following chapters of this book demonstrate teacher research thinking, as introduced below.

1.3 Summary of Each Chapter

Chapters 2–8 of this book provide background and context that provides authentic entry into understanding teachers' ways of engaging in research thinking in each context. In each chapter, research methodology, data and analysis are followed by a discussion of the research thinking evident. Section 1 focuses on in-service educators (I-STs, UEs and TEs), Section 2 on PSTs, and both emphasise research thinking for responsive teaching.

PSTs, I-STs, UE's and TEs experiences and contexts are crucial to understand the research undertaken in this book. Therefore Chap. 2 proves research vignettes based on participant observation data and Chaps. 3–6 include vignettes, stories of experience to provide a strong sense of context. Chapter 7 explains the Indonesian education context to readers who may be otherwise unfamiliar and Chap. 8 provides extensive description of the curriculum context.

1.3.1 Section 1: In-Service Educators

Section 1 pertains to practicing educators, with Chap. 2 focusing on an I-ST and his classroom practice, Chaps. 3 and 4 on I-STs enrolled in Master's degrees and Chap. 5 is on UE and TE research thinking. Chapter 2 is first in the sequence because it emphasises the influence of practicing teachers' research thinking on school students and demonstrates high levels of teacher autonomy in the classroom. Chapter 2 also brings together the audience and focus of this book, demonstrating the interactions between I-ST, PST and UE that are enabled by the RSD. Chapters 3 and 4 provide exemplars of how the research thinking of practicing teachers enrolled in Master's degrees may be developed. These degrees facilitate research thinking by engaging classroom teachers in sophisticated assessment tasks with a variety of levels of autonomy when developing open-access resources (Chap. 3) and research publications (Chap. 4). Chapter 5 then looks at how UEs, themselves teachers of undergraduate and Master's courses, may have their research thinking enhanced in Educational Development programs.

In Chap. 2, Home, an I-ST, Snelling, then a PST and Willison, a TE report a research-based learning context in *High School Student Experiences of Teacher Research Thinking,* set in a geographically remote, resource-poor school in Australia. This chapter presents a Participant Observation study, conducted by the PST, of the I-ST's explicit facilitation of student research skills in a combined Year 9/10 subject named 'Impact' by the school. The data is presented as research vignettes, stories of teacher and student engagement in the classroom of 20 students. The focus of the vignettes is student involvement in teacher-guided tasks intended to facilitate student research skills and builds on the I-ST's earlier work (Home, 2017). The nature of the I-ST's research thinking is expounded, and the research skills of students that are evident in his classroom emphasised. It is the chapter's explication of influence on school students that is most crucial because the number one aim of all teacher education is to enable higher quality school student learning than would be the case without it.

In Chap. 3 Brown and colleagues from The University of Calgary, Canada, write about *Open Educational Practices (OEP) for Research Skill Development with In-service School Teachers.* Building on their earlier findings (Jacobsen et al., 2018) the authors describe how post-secondary instructors use open educational practices and layered assignments, feedback loops, and assessment to engage I-STs enrolled in graduate degrees in making research thinking explicit and accessible to a broader professional and academic audience beyond the duration of a course or program. The RSD conceptual framework is used to demonstrate how open educational practices can be used to facilitate research-based skills for examining meaningful problems of practice and engaging in a scholarly community of inquiry. The authors present their findings with two groups of graduate students (n = 24) and share results about their experiences with open educational practices in the graduate program and implications for I-ST.

Chapter 4 *Exploring In-service Teacher-Researcher Reflexivity: Education Research as Cultural work* is by Heck from the University of the Sunshine Coast, Australia. Heck considers how the prevalent technical view of educational research that provides generalisable solutions of 'what works' has compounded the distance between theory and practice. She adapts a cultural role for educational research which recognises I-STs as practitioner-researchers. Building on previous research (Heck et al., 2020) Heck's chapter examines a Teacher Educator's use of the RSD in the first semester of a Master's program to facilitate nine I-STs' reflective engagement in topics that deepened their pedagogy or practice and was a pathway to a professional publication. The implications of this work provide scope for researchers and practitioners to engage in dialogue that counters the sole focus on a technical 'what works' view of educational research and opens up new ways of working, thinking and researching in classrooms.

In Chap. 5 Tiala and Loy lay out *Research-Oriented University Instruction: The Research Skill Development framework and Communities of Practice* in their respective universities in Midwestern United States and on the Canadian prairies. In this chapter, the authors describe how the RSD was used in educational development for UEs. The authors found that to make lasting and meaningful change to classroom instruction, it was valuable to engage and sustain instructors as a community-of-practice or network that can learn and evolve their practice together over a period of time. For communities of practice, the RSD framework can spark interest, provide common language, interrogate existing practices and envision alternative possibilities in teaching, and catalyse individual and group Scholarship of Teaching and Learning (SoTL). Building on their previous work (Guo et al., 2018; Tiala, 2017) and based on the perspectives and data provided by the authors' and members of their professional networks, this chapter positions the RSD as a valuable and strategic tool. The authors found the RSD useful for mitigating difficult problems by enabling flexible communities of practice to respond to and influence changing priorities across teaching, learning, research, and student-engagement mandates.

1.3.2 Section 2: Preservice Teachers' Research Thinking

Chapters 6 and 7 are rich in PST research thinking developed in digital contexts, where the former depicts a quick response to COVID pandemic-induced distance learning provision, using social media to which students already had access. The latter provides a more proactive and long-term planned response using Learning Management Systems and various media, so together these chapters capture digitally responsive teachers' research thinking. Chapter 8 has a focus on the richness of student learning enabled by Curriculum-based Undergraduate Research Experiences (CUREs) whether online, face-to-face or blended modes. Across Chaps. 6–8, Preservice teachers engage in University assignments that are structured to, and require, a variety of levels of research autonomy.

In Chap. 6 Mataniari and colleagues from Jambi University, Indonesia discuss *Preservice Teachers' Use of Social Media for the Development of Their Research Skills.* The authors build on previous work (Mataniari et al., 2020) and present their findings about developing PST research thinking through social media as guided by the RSD and used with 67 students in a second-year education course. In the chapter they explain how they scaffolded the development of digital learning strategies for interactive learning through widely-used online social media platforms. The outcomes of their study suggest that PSTs who develop research thinking through digital learning strategies show potential as curriculum designers who, as future school teachers, will have the capacity to create innovative social media-based interactive learning models for nurturing their own students' research skills.

In digitally-related work in a very different cultural zone, McLeod from Monash University, Australia, follows on in Chap. 7 with *Digital Skill Mythology and Understanding in Preservice Teachers.* McLeod notes that increase in complexity and importance of digital skills in society is not correlated with students' actual development of commensurate skills, despite the myth about students being 'Digital Natives'. That myth, she argues, leads to a down-playing of the need for explicit teaching of digital skills so that when these PSTs go on to become I-STs, they encounter the same assumptions as at university, leading to 'double jeopardy digital inequity'

(McLay & Reyes, 2019). McLeod explains how the digital skills implicit in the Research Skill Development Framework (RSD) were articulated in the Digital Skill Development (DSD) framework that she collaboratively devised for Monash University (McLeod & Torres, 2020; Pilz et al., 2021). McLeod presents data from a large metropolitan Australian University and compares self-reported digital skills of 219 PSTs with their demonstrated understanding of what digital skills encompass. Findings show which DSD skills PSTs recognised and which needed more focus in the unit of study, and provides the reader with strategies for their own diagnosis.

Palmer from the College of New Jersey (TCNJ), a public Liberal Arts University in the USA, looks beyond digital environments in Chap. 8 to discuss *Undergraduate Research for Preservice Teachers: Navigating its Rich Complexity and Novel Possibilities*. Palmer overviews student participation in targeted curriculum-based undergraduate research experiences (CUREs) threaded throughout the PST programs at TCNJ. The chapter then reports on the results of a qualitative case study of a teacher educator's approach to facilitating a research-integrated second-year pre-clinical adolescent psychology course in a secondary teacher education program. Palmer finds that student investment in research and future-oriented thinking creates robust pathways to their professional communities. There is also corroborating evidence of PST's capacity to persist across multiple learning environments where robust coursework opportunities for frequent rehearsal and iterations ensured the incorporation of integrated research thinking into habits of mind. Palmer concludes that CUREs enable students to identify themselves as generative thinkers, autonomous learners, and prideful teacher-advocates.

1.4 This Book's Contribution to Education Theory, Practice and Research

This book shows how responsive teachers are consumers *and* producers of research. As consumers, teachers draw on and discerningly adapt an evidence base that includes educational research literature and conference presentations, and from which they must extract meaning, consider others' ideas, and apply information judiciously to their classes. Decoding others' evidence bases, and the explicit or implicit theories of education that underpin these also requires teachers to make connections between theory and practice, known as research translation. As producers of research they generate pertinent data, determine what is effective and consolidate that as well as determine what needs to change. Adapting innovatively to students' learning needs and to contingencies poses the risk of disregarding existing good features of teaching, so approaches that discern what needs to stay and what needs to change are vital. Research thinking, activated through explicit development of educators' research skills, enables responsive teaching that consolidates, changes and connects practice.

This chapter characterised research thinking in terms of six forms of thinking associated with the research facets of the RSD comprising *Purposive Thinking, Informed*

Thinking, Astute Thinking, Harmonising Thinking, Insightful Thinking and *Externalised Thinking*. In big-picture terms, these are the forms of thinking that characterise not only research processes, but also evidence-based practice, critical thinking, problem solving, and digital literacy; this characterisation of research thinking can help educators and students see the connections between these otherwise disparate teaching and learning regimes. To enact effective change, consideration must be given to the ecology of learning, where changing one aspect of learning may have an impact on other key aspects. Responsive teachers perceive and understand the interconnectivity of the different components of the learning enterprise and so do not make changes without considering the broader context and interactions. Once changes are made, teachers also need to determine the value add and decide to consolidate, adapt or reject the changes.

The RSD facets and the associated research thinking characterised in this book can help make connections: between theory and practice; across physical and virtual classrooms; across subjects and disciplines for disciplinary thinking and for the highly interdisciplinary thinking required in Education; among often contending education theories and pedagogies, such as Direct Instruction and Discovery Learning; and between the different forms of research thinking listed above so that students are metacognitively aware of their growth. As an example, Chap. 2 evidences connections though RSD use between:

- PST, I-ST and UE
- teacher and high school student
- subjects as varied as Music and 'Impact'
- the years e.g., use with Year 5/6 and with Year 9/10
- and in different pedagogical stances, such as the Inquiry learning of the subject Impact and the content focus of Music

In a major contribution to research, the RSD framework accommodates the range of approaches teachers in schools and universities tend to draw on, regardless of framing by theorists, and so helps unearth otherwise hidden connections. The RSD's continuum of learning autonomy (Willison & O'Regan, 2007; Willison et al., 2017; Willison et al., 2020) provides a conceptual spectrum of possibilities for educational theory and practice and this continuum, therefore, can be used to guide and inspire research thinking that is mindful of a range of theoretical perspectives. This is a vital feature of the RSD, as it enables educators to be bricoleurs (Reilly, 2009) who make judgements about theory and piece together practice based on what is appropriate for their students.

While the RSD has been examined extensively for Higher Education in various disciplines, the evidence of effective use of the RSD in teacher education and for impact on school student learning is sparse. This book represents an important move to an evidence base in the neglected area of schooling to determine to what extent:

- PSTs develop research thinking
- I-STs enact research thinking

- I-STs' research thinking is maintained and enhanced through professional development
- RSD use facilitates research thinking that enables teachers to be responsive to their students' needs and improve student learning.

Each chapter is a content-rich microcosm where research skill development is implemented to promote responsive teaching. Individually, the chapters provide evidence of effective use by TEs of diverse approaches. What binds the chapters together and provides a holistic and profound sense of enlargement across education is their use of the RSD framework. Explicit research skill development, broadly perceived, shows great potential to enable teacher research thinking through which teachers are enabled to be responsive to the immediate, mid and long-term demands of their profession.

1.5 Conclusion

Research thinking enables responsive teaching that consolidates, changes and connects learning and teaching. The Research Skill Development framework can be used to facilitate such multi-faceted research thinking that is purposeful, informed, astute, harmonising, insightful and externalised. Research thinking is vital to deal with the complexities of being and becoming teachers who are not merely reactive, but are responsive, identifying not only what to change but what to consolidate as they see their part in the connections across all of student learning.

The chapters of this book show how educators from PST, I-ST and UE have applied the Research Skill Development framework and research thinking to make consolidations, changes and connections in their practice. The shared conceptualisation of the Research Skill Development framework has come to fruition in the research thinking that enables teachers to be responsive, striving to facilitate their students' own purposeful, informed, astute, harmonising, insightful and externalised thinking.

References

Brew, A. (2013). Understanding the scope of undergraduate research: A framework for curricular and pedagogical decision-making. *Higher Education, 66*(5), 603–618.

Brew, A., & Saunders, C. (2020). Making sense of research-based learning in teacher education. *Teaching and Teacher Education, 87*, 102935.

Chin, C. (2006). Classroom interaction in science: Teacher questioning and feedback to students' responses. *International Journal of Science Education, 28*(11), 1315–1346.

Cranton, P. (2011). A transformative perspective on the scholarship of teaching and learning. *Higher Education Research and Development, 30*(1), 75–86.

De Vos, M. E., Baartman, L. K. J., Van Der Vleuten, C. P. M., & De Bruijn, E. (2019). Exploring how educators at the workplace inform their judgement of students' professional performance. *Journal of Education and Work, 32*(8), 693–706.

Dewey, J. (1910). *What is thought?* D.C. Heath & Co.

Etymologyonline. (no date). https://www.etymonline.com/search?q=skill

Fryer, D. (2022). The models of engaged learning and teaching (MELT): Connecting sophisticated thinking from early childhood to PhD (book review). *Journal of Interdisciplinary Studies in Education, 11*(1), 149–153.

Guo, X., Loy, K., & Banow, R. (2018). Can first-year undergraduate geography students do individual research? *Journal of Geography in Higher Education, 42*(3), 412–426.

Hallman, H. L., Rios, A., Craig, C. J., & Hill-Jackson, V. (2022). Teacher education's moment: From solution to challenge. *Journal of Teacher Education, 73*(2), 127–128.

Heck, D., Willis, A., Simon, S., Grainger, P., & Smith, K. (2020). Becoming a teacher: Scaffolding post-practicum reflection. In *Enriching higher education students' learning through post-work placement interventions* (pp. 173–188). Springer.

Home, J. (2017). Multidisciplinary approach to MELT use from Grade 5 to Year 12. In *Proceedings of the international conference on models of engaged learning and teaching*, Adelaide, 11–13 December. Retrieved February 25, 2022, from https://www.adelaide.edu.au/melt/ua/media/450/homeimelt2017paper.pdf

Jacobsen, M., McDermott, M., Brown, B., Eaton, S. E., & Simmons, M. (2018). Graduate students' research-based learning experiences in an online Master of Education program. *Journal of University Teaching and Learning Practice, 15*(4) (Article 4).

Kemmis, S. (2009). Action research as a practice-based practice. *Educational Action Research, 17*(3), 463–474.

Mataniari, R., Willison, J., Effendi Hasibuan, M. H., Sulistiyo, U., & Dewi, F. (2020). Portraying students' critical thinking skills through research skill development (RSD) framework: A case of a biology course in an Indonesian University. *Journal of Turkish Science Education, 17*(2), 302–314.

McLay, K. F., & Reyes, V. C. (2019). Identity and digital equity: Reflections on a university educational technology course. *Australasian Journal of Educational Technology, 35*(6), 15–29.

McLeod, A., & Torres, L. (2020, April). Enhancing first year university students' digital skills with the digital skill development (DSD) framework. In *Society for information technology & teacher education international conference* (pp. 373–379).

McNiff, J. (1995). *Action research for professional development* (pp. 137–151). Hyde.

Moser, S., Zumbach, J., & Deibl, I. (2017). The effect of metacognitive training and prompting on learning success in simulation-based physics learning. *Science Education, 101*(6), 944–967.

Pilz, S., McLeod, A., & Yazbeck, B. (2021). Transforming practice through digital skills development. In *Connecting the library to the curriculum* (pp. 211–227). Springer.

Reilly, M. A. (2009). Opening spaces of possibility: The teacher as bricoleur. *Journal of Adolescent and Adult Literacy, 52*(5), 376–384.

Rinatovna, K. L. (2017). Psychological and pedagogical foundations of undergraduates' research thinking development process. *Procedia-Social and Behavioral Sciences, 237*, 1405–1411.

Scherpereel, C. M., Williams, S. K., & Hoefle, S. (2022). The difficulties of context: An exploratory study of learning transfer from a business simulation game. *Decision Sciences Journal of Innovative Education, 20*(2), 89–101.

Spronken-Smith, R., Brodeur, J., Kajaks, T., Luck, M., Myatt, P., Verburgh, A., Walkington, H., & Wuetherick, B. (2013). Completing the research cycle: A framework for promoting dissemination of undergraduate research and inquiry. *Teaching and Learning Inquiry: The ISSOTL Journal, 1*(2), 105–118.

Tiala, S. (2017). A facilitator's reaction to implementing the RSD in a community of practice. In The *conference proceedings of the international conference on the models of engaged learning and teaching* (I-MELT), Adelaide, Australia, 11–13 December, 2017. https://www.adelaide.edu.au/melt/ua/media/378/tialaimelt2017paper.pdf

Willcoxson, L., Manning, M. L., Johnston, N., & Gething, K. (2011). Enhancing the research-teaching Nexus: Building teaching-based research from research-based teaching. *International Journal of Teaching and Learning in Higher Education, 23*(1), 1–10.

Willison, J. (2020a). *The models of engaged learning and teaching: Connecting sophisticated learning from early childhood to Ph.D.* Springer.

Willison, J. (2020b). Blended learning needs blended evaluation. In *Critical perspectives on teaching, learning and leadership* (pp. 87–106). Springer.

Willison, J. W. (2012). When academics integrate research skill development in the curriculum. *Higher Education Research & Development, 31*(6), 905–919.

Willison, J. W. (2018). Research skill development spanning higher education: Critiques, curricula and connections. *Journal of University Teaching and Learning Practice, 15*(4), 1.

Willison, J., & Buisman-Pijlman, F. (2016). PhD prepared: Research skill development across the undergraduate years. *International Journal for Researcher Development, 7*(1).

Willison, J., & O'Regan, K. (2007). Commonly known, commonly not known, totally unknown: A framework for students becoming researchers. *Higher Education Research and Development, 26*(4), 393–409.

Willison, J., Sabir, F., & Thomas, J. (2017). Shifting dimensions of autonomy in students' research and employment. *Higher Education Research and Development, 36*(2), 430–443.

Willison, J., Zhu, X., Xie, B., Yu, X., Chen, J., Zhang, D., Shashoug, I., & Sabir, F. (2020). Graduates' affective transfer of research skills and evidence-based practice from university to employment in clinics. *BMC Medical Education, 20*(1), 1–18.

Wilmore, M., & Willison, J. (2016). Graduates' attitudes to research skill development in undergraduate media education. *Asia Pacific Media Educator, 26*(1), 113–128.

Zuber-Skerritt, O. (2002). The concept of action learning. *The Learning Organization, 9*(3), 114–124.

John Willison is the Director of the Bachelor of Teaching at the University of Adelaide and a National Senior Teaching Fellow. He was a secondary school science teacher for 10 years using systematic approaches to improving his students learning. He has researched how teachers develop their students' research skills and other forms of sophisticated thinking for three decades.

Open Access This chapter is licensed under the terms of the Creative Commons Attribution 4.0 International License (http://creativecommons.org/licenses/by/4.0/), which permits use, sharing, adaptation, distribution and reproduction in any medium or format, as long as you give appropriate credit to the original author(s) and the source, provide a link to the Creative Commons license and indicate if changes were made.

The images or other third party material in this chapter are included in the chapter's Creative Commons license, unless indicated otherwise in a credit line to the material. If material is not included in the chapter's Creative Commons license and your intended use is not permitted by statutory regulation or exceeds the permitted use, you will need to obtain permission directly from the copyright holder.

Part I
In-service Teachers' Research Thinking

Chapter 2
High School Student Experiences of Teacher Research Thinking

Jason Home, Tom Snelling, and John Willison

Abstract This chapter reports a Participant Observation study of a teacher's explicit facilitation of student research skills in a combined Year 9/10 subject that was designed to prepare students for a subsequent year-long *Research Project*. The Research Skill Development framework was used by the teacher to inform his planning for students' learning when they conducted their research. The setting is a geographically remote Kindergarten to Year 12 school in Australia, with very limited resources. The data, collected by a Preservice Teacher, is presented as research vignettes, stories of student engagement in the classroom. The focus of the vignettes and subsequent discussion is the teacher's research thinking and students' experiences of the development of their research skills in the classroom.

2.1 Introduction

This chapter reports on a participant observation study of a geographically remote Year 9/10 classroom in which the teacher used the Research Skill Development framework (RSD: Willison & O'Regan, 2007: see Chap. 1 for details) to plan and to facilitate student thinking. Representing the educators who are the subject of this book, the three authors of the chapter are Home, an In-Service Teacher (I-ST), Snelling, a Preservice Teacher (PST) at the time he collected the data and Willison, a University Educator whose role was specifically as a Teacher Educator (TE).

First the rationale of developing student research thinking is presented, and then the reasons the teacher, Home, chose to use the RSD to facilitate this thinking. Next,

---

J. Home (✉)
Victor Harbor High School, Victor Harbor, Australia
e-mail: Jason.Home553@schools.sa.edu.au

T. Snelling
Mercedes College, Adelaide, Australia

J. Willison
University of Adelaide, Adelaide, Australia
e-mail: john.willison@adelaide.edu.au

© The Author(s) 2024
J. Willison (ed.), *Research Thinking for Responsive Teaching*,
SpringerBriefs in Education, https://doi.org/10.1007/978-981-99-6679-0_2

the participant observation methodology of the study used by Snelling is followed by research vignettes of the classroom observations across two lessons. The chapter then discusses the evidence for Home's research thinking, and his facilitation of student research skills and their consequent classroom experiences. Implications for research and teaching conclude the chapter.

2.2 Rationale for Secondary School Student Research Skills

In order to make an explicit, national shift from a school-system focused on content and recall (Renzulli, 2000) the Australian Curriculum from 2012 foregrounded the development of student thinking (Australian Curriculum, Assessment and Reporting Authority, no date). This thinking is now characterised in the 8th iteration of the curriculum as '…productive, purposeful and intentional [and] is at the centre of effective learning. By applying a sequence of thinking skills, students develop an increasingly sophisticated understanding of the processes they can use whenever they encounter problems, unfamiliar information and new ideas.' (Australian Curriculum, Assessment and Reporting Authority, n.d.). Such a characterisation was at the heart of the RSD when it was developed 15 years ago.

The Australian Curriculum includes *inquiring* as an approach to a core capability of *critical and creative thinking*, where students '… pose questions and identify and clarify information and ideas, and then organise and process information. They use questioning to investigate and analyse ideas and issues, make sense of and assess information and ideas, and collect, compare and evaluate information from a range of sources.' (Australian Curriculum, Assessment and Reporting Authority, n.d.). These skills were particularly important in the state in which this research took place, because the senior secondary curriculum required a senior high school *Research Project* of five months or more duration. However, critiques suggest a deficiency in the development of high school student research skills (Lazonder & Harmsen, 2016).

This research is set in a geographically remote town, and while Australia is viewed to be a highly urbanised nation, four million people (31% of the Australian workforce) are located outside of urban centres (Department of Jobs and Small Business, 2019). The lack of thinking skill development is felt across the nation, but rural communities are further disadvantaged in this area, as they are more likely to cater to low socioeconomic families that are disadvantaged in terms of educational resources and outcomes (McCourt & Ikutegbe, 2019). Rural and geographically remote students must be taught, in ways that are relevant to them, the skills they need to thrive in school and later in life, including the thinking used in research processes.

Learning through research can be taught implicitly or explicitly in Inquiry-based learning (IBL). Research skills can be implicitly developed in the classroom by "embracing a question-centred pedagogy" where the responsibility for asking questions is shifted from the teacher to the students (Sciacca, 2016, p. 6). However, unguided IBL environments have been reported to cause "a much larger cognitive load and led to poorer learning" while explicit and guided instruction produce better results in regard to problem solving skills (Kirschner et al., 2006, p. 80). Hmelo-Silver et al. (2007) argue a third option, that guided instruction should be the foundation on which unguided inquiry learning occurs, and that students are better able to develop lifelong skills if both methods of instructions are used in concert (de Jong, et al., 2023). This view implies a shift over time from explicit to implicit instruction of IBL.

While the development of research skills is deemed valuable for learning by the Australian Curriculum, the difficulty for educators lies in knowing how to teach these skills and making them seem relevant to students and other teachers, principals and parents. The development of thinking skills is difficult and requires students to be active and persistent learners; student attitudes towards learning presents the greatest enablers and barriers to engagement in sophisticated thinking development (Malik et al., 2018; Willingham, 2019). One of the numerous challenges is shown by one study where the majority of students did not see the relevance of the thinking skills learned because they saw their educational goal was '…achieving a high score for Year 12 studies and thus entry to university' (Grainger et al., 2019: 441).

2.2.1 Context and Why RSD in the Year 9/10 Class

This study was undertaken at a Government K-12 area school in a remote mining town in Australia. The school's full-time teaching staff numbered 25 at the time of data gathering (2019), and there were 215 enrolled students (ACARA, 2018). The Index of Community Socio-Educational Advantage (ICSEA) of the school was below average (ACARA, 2018) and 60% had a language background other than English (ACARA, 2018). Observations took place in a class comprising Year 9 and 10 students that was focussing on the development of research skills.

In order to complete the State's Year 11 and 12 Curriculum, all students must, as noted above, pass a major, half year-long *Research Project*, typically conducted in Year 11. However, Home and a colleague in the school who taught the *Research Project* found that students often struggled to put together a complete and coherent project. These individual projects were tedious for students and staff involved, with the focus often becoming 'how do we get them over the line?', rather than developing and showcasing students' effective research skills.

Home was interested in exploring the use of the RSD, introduced three years earlier in his PST program by the TE Willison, and saw the framework may assist with the identified difficulties of student engagement with the Research Project. School leadership gave approval for Jason to co-develop a new subject, *Impact*, which was designed to introduce and develop student research skills in keeping with the RSD. The pedagogical premise was that students had the capacity for sophisticated thinking, however, systemic failures of the education system in part due to the 'tyranny of distance' (Rossi & Sirna, 2008) left students with little tangible and relatable experience in engaging in research and inquiry learning. Epistemic justice is needed to overcome the structural inequity for the students, by providing practices that can empower and give due credit to student ability and agency (Fricker, 2003). Through the explicit teaching and usage of the RSD framework, the intention was that students would explore the six facets of research in different contexts, building these skills through years 9 and 10, to meet the academic rigours of *Research Project* in their final years of schooling. The research questions of this study are:

(1) What is the nature of Home's research thinking in the classroom?
(2) What are student experiences of explicit research skill development in Home's *Impact* class?

2.3 Methodology

In order to capture the richness of student experience of Home's research thinking and facilitation of their research skills, participant observation methodology was used by Snelling as both PST and researcher in the classroom, to learn about the activities of a whole class in their natural setting (Kawulich, 2005). As participant observer he established a rapport with the class in order to obtain rich and detailed data (Bernard, 1994). Participant observation is a valuable method of data collection when the researcher maintains a non-judgemental attitude, is a good listener, and is interested in learning more about others (DeWalt & DeWalt, 1998). Furthermore, Snelling's positioning as a participant observer in a research scenario made it possible for him to observe and interact with members of the studied group without disrupting the typical interactions of the group in question (Adler & Adler, 1994). In the classroom, the researcher (Snelling) was introduced to the students, who were given an overview of the scope of the study, and the types of questions which they may be asked. Snelling as researcher made notes throughout the lesson in a notebook about events that occurred in the classroom that suggested student interaction with the RSD, and informal conversations in the classroom about their experiences while engaged in learning tasks were also recorded in a notebook. Willison, as TE and research supervisor, was present in the first classroom observation to provide Snelling extra guidance about his field notes after the lesson, then left the town. From Snelling's observation data, two vignettes were written in first-person and independent of Home, but were shared with him on the writing of this chapter. Home chose to use his own first name and made no changes to the vignettes presented as he felt they captured the classroom as he remembered it, in keeping with the quality standard of member checking (Birt et al., 2016). Student names and the company acronym used in the vignettes are pseudonyms.

Ethics approval for this research project was granted by the Human Research Ethics Committee prior to the commencement of the four-day observation period. Prior to the researcher's arrival to the area in which the school was located, the school distributed parent/guardian consent forms detailing the purpose of the project, the reasons for which they were involved in the project and alerting the participants that they were free at any time to withdraw from the project. Informal conversations in the classroom were only held with students that returned a completed consent form prior to the first observation period.

2.3.1 Data Analysis Methodology

The two vignettes were analysed with reference to:

(1) The Research Thinking characterised in Table 1.1 of Chap. 1, to determine the nature of Home's research thinking in the classroom, addressing Question 1.
(2) The six facets of the RSD, introduced in Chap. 1, to determine the student classroom experience of Home's research thinking, addressing Question 2.

The Vignettes were subject to deep reading, using these two analytical tools (Research Thinking and the RSD facets) to identify text that directly related to the research questions. Next, exemplifying statements were chosen from the vignettes to insightfully represent the teacher research thinking and the student research experiences respectively. As exemplifying statements, they are not representative of the classroom experience, but rather shed light on possibilities for teaching and learning. An example of a 'Lotus Diagram', referred to in Vignette 2 may be found here https://www.edrawmax.com/article/what-is-lotus-diagram.html.

2.4 Results

2.4.1 Vignette 1: Climate Change Source Analysis

Jason announces the start of *Impact*, with students moving in ones and twos to collect their materials for class. Several students wait for Jason to provide them with writing utensils. There's an easy rapport between the teacher and the students, and there is a general din of conversation. The class settles into the task at hand, copying down a fictional quotation from the board.

Jason states that the focus of *Impact* today is source analysis on the causes of global warming. The paragraph the students are copying was authored by Jason but credited to author 'Croaky McToadface', the Vice President of a fabricated mining company BJK. Croaky refutes the evidence of climate change in the text. There are a pair of spelling mistakes two thirds of the way through the paragraph.

Jason announces that the students' task for the moment is to analyse the paragraph on the board. They are given a few minutes to copy the text in their own books and circle statements that support or detract from the overall argument. While the majority of the class settles into relative quiet, two students have pulled out their phones.

After five minutes have passed, Jason asks the class what they have come up with. One student, Alex, immediately throws up his hand to assert that the statement "trees need carbon dioxide to live" is the only factual statement. Riley states that the argument that "we need to pump out more carbon" is 'sooo wrong'. One student Jordan states that the same phrase is "twisting the facts". Jason waits for several seconds for more answers, but the class remains quiet. Jason asks if the students know what 'BJK' is. Several joke answers are provided including "Big Jumping Kangaroo", but it is Jason who provides the correct answer. Jason then asks the students to reflect on what effect the authorship has on the trustworthiness of the source. One student calls out "bias".

Finally, Jason points out the two misspellings in the paragraph he has written on the board. Most students claim that they believed these were genuine mistakes on his part, and not placed there to bring in to question the credibility of the source. The students then assert that the source that has been presented to them is not useful. Jason asks them to reflect on why they believe this, before calling a short break.

After stretching their legs for ten minutes, the students return. Jason explains that the students need to take what they have learnt in the initial sources analysis and do the same work again with additional sources that are provided to them. Varying levels of analysis of the sources occur around the classroom, ranging from scrutinising the quality of the handwriting on one page, to the website URL on another, and a handful of students questioning whether an individual's qualifications make that person a reliable source. Jason asks a small group of students which facets of the RSD are being used in the work they are tasked with. The group pauses for a moment to think, and they eventually respond with "find and generate", and "analyse and synthesise".

After Jason asks Riley how she is going with the task, she responds, "I hate analysing!". She has only circled two statements on the page at this time. However, Riley is so far the only student who has questioned whether a Ph.D. in Physics is relevant to question the science behind climate change. As the lesson draws to a close, only two or three students are still actively engaging with the content of the lesson.

2.4.2 Vignette 2: Australia Day Date Questions

Students rise from their seats and collect books, laptops and printed notes from around the room. Those towards the front of the class make a start to their work, while those at the back were either absent or inattentive during yesterday's lesson. Jason steps outside to deal with a pair of students' behaviours, and one student from the back row asks another if the work for today is to be done on the task sheet or on their laptops. While this is taking place, a student at the front of the classroom attempts to draw me into a spirited conversation with other students about his sandwich filling.

Jason returns inside and introduces the topic of determining and refining a question. Students are to fill out a Lotus Diagram to work out the complexities of the 'Change the Date' debate on the national holiday Australia Day, which falls on 26th January. A variety of opinions are spontaneously called out around the classroom.

Riley and her table partner are discussing the date of Australia Day and are both in favour of keeping it as it is. 'If you don't want it to be on that day, then don't celebrate it', she says.

At a nearby table, Peyton, Alex and Jordan are discussing the origin of Australia Day, and when it could be moved to. Peyton states that 'Australia Day is the day that First Nations people got rights from the government'. Neither of his table neighbours nor he verify this information.

Alex asks 'Is it possible to move *Australia Day* to *National Sorry Day*?'.

Jordan responds: 'They could change the name to *Revolution Day*'.

'If we call it *Invasion Day*, doesn't that mean that we did something bad?' asks Alex.

These students appear to have already come to the conclusion that the date for *Australia Day* needs to be changed or it should be renamed, rather than choosing and refining a question about the topic.

Taylor, Alex, Jordan and Peyton begin to fill out their Lotus Diagrams. One box is labelled 'Date', with examples such as the 25th of January, the 27th of January, and May 8th filled in by the students. I enquire about the latter; it is a reference to Australians being mates.

Taylor asks Alex 'Would *Colonisation Day* be a suitable replacement for *Australia Day*? He searches for the definition of 'colonisation' and believes that he is on to something when he discovers that the definition for the word fits the actions of the Europeans that migrated to Australia.

There are ten minutes left now until the end of class. Jason calls the students attention to the front and asks them to refine the research they have been doing into a research question. The attention of the students begins to wane, some pulling out their phones, and others engaging in conversation. Peyton and Alex are the only students that participate in this final task for the lesson. They have refined their research into one question, 'Why should we celebrate Australia Day?'.

The following analysis of the two research vignettes makes the evidence for each facet of Jason's research thinking explicit. The following section shows the experiences of students when he is facilitating the development of their research skills. The names used in the vignette are used throughout the discussion, to be consistent with the vignette data e.g. Jason rather than Home.

2.5 Discussion

2.5.1 The Classroom Teacher's Research Thinking

Two-and-a-half years after completing his teaching degree, what is the nature of Jason's research thinking in the Year 9/10 classroom as analysed with the facets presented in Chap. 1?

2.5.1.1 Purposive Thinking

With reference to the RSD facets, Jason's prime and explicit teaching purpose in the two vignettes is to facilitate student engagement in 'source analysis' and 'choosing and refining a question', a specific aspect of embark and clarify. He states each at the beginning of a lesson as a learning intention for students. With clarity of direction, Jason is equipped to know if, when and how a lesson may need to be modified to better achieve the learning intended, or even if other, better opportunities for students could be pursued in a responsive manner.

Jason's purpose to guide the students' explicit development of research skills is shown in the vignette when he 'asks a small group of students which facets of the RSD are being used in the work they are tasked with. The group pauses for a moment to think, though they eventually respond with "find and generate", and "analyse and synthesise".' While research skill development can be left to occur implicitly in inquiry-based learning, Jason seeks for students to know and articulate explicitly which facets they are focussing on.

2.5.1.2 Informed Thinking

Informed thinking makes opportunities to not only be informed by frameworks, sources, conferences and colleagues, but treats as prime data students' classroom experiences. Walking around and chatting to students is arguably the most insightful data of all, especially given Jason has clear purposive thinking that helps him know how to respond to student needs. His information and data for informed thinking includes getting to know the students and staff at the school and the deficits in the curriculum.

In the classroom, Jason talks with students individually, in small groups and the large group. After some questions and a few student answers 'Jason waits for several seconds for more answers, but his class remains quiet.' This is a cue to Jason that some students may need more guidance and prompting with evaluation of the source. He then moves to check if students even know what BJK stands for, and gains some humorous student ideation, such as *Big Jumping Kangaroo*. Since the students didn't know that BJK was a mining company, his subsequent guiding question about authorship would make little sense. Student silence and unfilled answer spaces are forms of data that impacts on and guides responsive teaching.

2.5.1.3 Astute Thinking

Jason evaluates classroom information on a minute-by-minute basis. This includes evaluating a student yawn, to determine if this is an indication of wider-scale flagging or a one-off. Jason is especially evaluating students' work to determine where different groups of individuals are up to and this evaluation helps him determine what to do next. His evaluation of the comic names, mentioned above, prompted

Jason to spell out what BJK stands for. Astute thinking does not believe by default but weighs-up and checks. Astute thinking also reflects afterwards to determine lessons learned, including what could have been done better and what went better than expected. This is in keeping with Schön's (1987) focus of teachers reflecting back to times of uncertainty in a classroom when, in the midst of action, they decided responsively what to do. This is where the teacher teaches themselves about their own enacted responsiveness, and learns lessons from their responses, whether effective or ineffective. Jason's practice is also in keeping with the very different notion of Brookfield's (2017) reflection, which emphasises breaking down one's own prejudices and bringing in others' perspective, exampled by Jason's use of the RSD as well as other literature.

2.5.1.4 Harmonising Thinking

There are clear challenges with managing the classroom, including students chatting, off-task phone use and eventual tedium. Early in Vignette 1 'there's an easy rapport between the teacher and the students, and there is a general din of conversation.' A large part of Jason's management is maintaining rapport with students, and he uses humour devices such as the persona *Croaky McToadface*, perhaps prompting students to be comfortable with providing joke answers of their own. Students even give leeway to Jason, when they noted spelling mistakes in the board text but did not point them out or blame him because 'they believed these were genuine mistakes on his part'.

Part of rapport is to maintain a positive learning environment even when the conceptual demands are high. Students '…are given a few minutes to copy the text in their own books…'. While board copying as an instructional strategy is frowned on, Jason's purpose for student copying off the board is thoughtful. Here, student copying is an enabling feature, giving students who are easily disrupted a focussed activity that they can be successful at, before moving to the hard conceptual work, in which many may struggle. That Jason eases students into a task through copying is a teaching choice is demonstrated by contrasting it with Vignette 2, where students have access to laptops and printouts; the copying activity is a considered responsiveness after getting to know the students. In this geographically remote context with limited resourcing, including difficulties with effective diagnosis of learning disorders, starting simple may have had profound positive influence on gaining students engagement in the chief and sophisticated purpose that is built on this copying activity: analysis.

Jason also manages the energy levels in the room, sensing times that students need a break and then responding appropriately by providing '10 min spent outside'. After a refreshing break, Jason introduces the next topic and there is an energised discussion about 'Australia Day', requiring all facets of student research thinking as shown in the next section.

2.5.1.5 Insightful Thinking

Jason's capacity to analyse needs and synthesise answers, fuelled by his creativity, gave him insights into what to craft. In the resources in the vignettes, he did not start from scratch, but synthesised new solutions from component parts, drawing on the facets of the RSD, and moulding and fitting them to the purpose. Jason uses the self-authored, semi-humorous source in part because he discerned that students in his *Impact* class would resonate with and be motivated by that style, rather than drier articles that they ultimately review later in the class. He may be wrong, and his insightful thinking will be on the lookout for his own misreading of the students.

2.5.1.6 Externalised Thinking

Jason's *pushed out* thinking is shown by his clear statement to the class about learning intentions for each lesson and, perhaps even more profoundly, the shared use of RSD facets to provide students with a big picture for their learning. This is Jason's decision to use explicit strategies as a preference over facilitating tacit learning. Moreover, class and group conversations stimulate Jason's thinking, for example causing him to realising for the first time in three years at the school that the students are not aware of what BJK is. This conversation-based realisation *pushes in* to Jason's teaching and causes him to, uncharacteristically, tell the students the answer.

2.5.2 Students' Experiences of Explicit Research Skill Development

The following analysis shows excerpts from the vignettes that epitomise student use of each of the six RSD facets to engage with source analysis in Vignette 1 and develop a researchable question in Vignette 2. There are multiple instances where only one or two students are so engaging with a specific facet, and there is no sense that this engagement extends to the whole class.

2.5.2.1 Students Embark and Clarify

In Vignette 2 the lesson is structured to facilitate student research question formation through a process that first unpacked a complex range of opinions about *Australia Day*. During the lesson, one student asks 'Is it possible to move Australia Day to National Sorry Day?' Another questions 'If we call it Invasion Day, doesn't that mean that we did something bad?' These are examples that reflect a synthesis of individual student thinking to determine a question, but one that is not 'refined'. They are both yes/no questions, even though the intent behind the questions is far richer than that.

When 'Jason calls the students attention to the front and asks them to refine the research they have been doing into a research question', he is striving to use their passion for the topic and new-found perspective to engage in the central purpose of the lesson. However, 'Peyton and Alex are the only students that participate in this final task for the lesson. They have refined the research into one question, "Why should we celebrate Australia Day?"' This is a clearly articulated and insightful question, and gets at underlying reasons for a celebration, which seems very sensible to ask before discussing 'whether to' and 'which date?' The vignette showcases Jason's process for facilitating student question posing but also shows the difficulties faced for most students to do so.

2.5.2.2 Students Find and Generate

Much that comes under 'finding' is considered to be unearthing sources and selecting appropriate ones. In the vignette, most sources are provided but student capacity to find is tested when they must '… circle statements that support or detract from the overall argument.' Here, finding information within a provided text is a complex skill in itself, involving a close reading of text for relevant information within a source. Strategies for finding information include identifying key terms, skimming, scanning and close reading. In Vignette 2, students do engage in finding sources, such as Peyton finding 'colonisation' is a term that perfectly fit their idea. One group, when asked, recognises that they are developing skills pertaining to "find and generate".

2.5.2.3 Students Evaluate and Reflect

Jason starts the lesson with a highly structured activity based on a source he wrote with intentional cues that cast doubt about its credibility, and several students called out answers that are effectively evaluative. Alex asserts that 'trees need carbon dioxide to live' is the only factual statement. Riley states that the argument that 'we need to pump out more carbon' is 'sooo wrong'. Jordan states that the same phrase is "twisting the facts". Overall, the class asserts 'that the source that has been presented to them is not useful' and indicate a 'bias' in the source.

The 'Croaky' source may have assisted student willingness to be discerning. The humour and glaring mistakes may have helped students get over 'source reverence' and be willing to find fault. As the class moves from this highly structured activity to subsequent ones with more choice, some students apply the evaluative criteria to website URLs and author qualifications

2.5.2.4 Students Organise and Manage

'In Vignette 2 Taylor, Alex, Jordan and Peyton begin to fill out their Lotus Diagrams. One box is labelled "Date", with the 25th of January, the 27th of January, and May 8th filled in.'

The organisational structure of Lotus Diagrams provides a format that facilitates broader thinking than students' current perspectives. From evaluate and reflect (above) the strategy to get students to pose and refine a question did not guarantee students moving out of their own self-referential perspectives. The spaces for different dates in the diagram show that different possibilities can be considered. This organisational structure enabled a shift from a 'yes–no' approach e.g., Celebrate on 26th January yes/no, to broadened possibilities. Teacher determined or student-determined organisational structures can provoke new conceptualisations of topics.

2.5.2.5 Students Analyse and Synthesise

In an interaction between two students, 'Taylor asks Alex "Would *Colonisation Day* be a suitable replacement for the title *Australia Day*?" He searches for the definition of 'colonisation' and believes that he is on to something when he discovers that the definition for the word fits the actions of the Europeans that migrated here.' Instead of engaging with the main direction of the class concerning date change, Taylor and Alex consider what happened on 26th January, 1788. Their excitement of renaming that date as *Colonisation Day* is because the word characterises, to them, the British actions of the time. Their example of question posing emerges from an explorative process requiring analysis of ideas and synthesis of discussion. While we tend to say that questions launch inquiry processes, if students are the posers, questions often may emerge over time and from much research thinking that draws on all the facets of the RSD. One student, Riley, states 'I hate analysing!' Analysis is conceptually difficult and perhaps required more modelling by Jason and practise with sources somewhat like the *Croaky McToadface* one. Nevertheless, one group perceives that the skills they are using include those needed to 'analyse and synthesise'.

2.5.2.6 Students Communicate and Apply

Communication is not explicitly stated by Jason as a learning intention, but the lesson demands and prompts high-level and frequent communication skills. Students are talking and listening in their small groups, with the conversation between Alex, Jordon and Peyton showing the students bouncing ideas off each other and growing in clarity and understanding. Moreover, they are writing and reading each other's work, such as the Lotus Diagram.

An indication of students applying what they learned previously is shown by the students' metacognition that recognised which facets of the RSD they were developing in particular during that lesson 'The group pauses for a moment to think, though they eventually respond with "find and generate", and "analyse and synthesise".

The above descriptions show how the teacher learning intention around analysing and synthesising and embarking and clarifying required other facets to be involved. Time and again, studies have shown that any sophisticated thinking, even if focussed on a specific facet such as analysis, is multifaceted (Ain et al., 2019; Willison, 2012; Willison et al., 2017, 2020; Wilmore & Willison, 2016) and this multifaceted thinking is evident for students and teacher in both vignettes. However, any approach to developing thinking skills must take the long view and may require 'at least three to five years of practice' (Willingham, 2019: 12). Thinking routines, which are learning heuristics, strategies and mental algorithms that teachers provide to students, have been recognised as a major value add by teachers over time (Ritchhart & Perkins, 2008). Students can draw on these thinking routines and apply them to areas outside of the context in which they were learned, and the RSD facets may be used by students in this way (Willison, 2020).

In addition, this case study shows the RSD may be a 'thinking routine' for teaching that provides guidance for thinking through deeply and planning for issues of concern. At the same time, the RSD may act as an heuristic to help teachers to respond quickly and appropriately to the immediate demands of a classroom, such as uncertaintly around 'BJK', or a student yawn. The exposure to the RSD for planning lessons was a factor in Jason being tuned to research thinking for considered, longer term planning. For the immediate needs of the classroom, further research is needed to see if a research-thinking heuristic does enable teachers to respond more effectively in the moment-by moment decision making that is reflection-in-action (Schon, 1988). If so, this would bring together two major thinkers on reflective practice, with Brookfield (2017) primarily focused on gaining perspective outside the one who is reflecting and Schön (1987) focused on the existing internal resources of the practitioner (Newman, 2020). Taken together these models of reflection imply the need for teachers to be tuned to finding out through externalised thinking and so professionally able to make internal decisions when the ways to proceed are unclear. Responsive teaching is engaged in by practitioners who use research approaches to find and generate optimum solutions and, when such research thinking is increasingly part of their mental repertoire, it improves the absolutely vital, quick decisions that all teachers make.

2.6 Conclusion

In-service teacher Home's use of the RSD provides a triple value-add. First, it guided Home's research thinking in response to students' needs in the lesson and unit design. Second, Home used it explicitly to guide students in the development of their research skills, in advance of a major research project in a subsequent year. And third,

Home modelled and demonstrated explicitly to Preservice Teacher Snelling research thinking for responsive teaching with the power of a shared articulation for students and teachers in the form of the RSD facets. Some students in Home's classes engaged with the RSD to interpret which facets they were currently focussing on, requiring and developing their metacognitive capacities. Willison as Teacher Educator introduced Home, when still a Preservice Teacher, to the RSD and now Home was introducing the framework to Snelling in a lived classroom experience. Snelling, as Preservice Teacher, experienced the RSD primarily in a classroom setting allowed him to see the strengths and weaknesses of its use. Taken together, the compounding effect of the RSD framework on high school students, Preservice Teacher, In-Service Teacher and Teacher Educator demonstrate its potential to empower educators with the kind of research thinking that enables their responsive teaching for engaged and sophisticated student learning.

References

Adler, P., & Adler, P. (1994). Observation techniques. in N. Denzin, & Y. Lincoln. *Handbook of qualitative research* (pp. 377–392). Sage.

Ain, C. T., Sabir, F., & Willison, J. (2019). Research skills that men and women developed at university and then used in workplaces. *Studies in Higher Education, 44*(12), 2346–2358.

Australian Curriculum, Assessment and Reporting Authority. (n.d.). *Australian curriculum: General capabilities; critical and creative thinking.* Retrieved from https://www.australiancurriculum.edu.au/f-10-curriculum/general-capabilities/critical-and-creative-thinking/

Australian Curriculum, Assessment and Reporting Authority. (2018). *My school.* https://www.myschool.edu.au [school's URL withheld].

Australian Jobs. (2019). Australian Government Department of Jobs and Small Business, viewed 12 November 2019. https://docs.employment.gov.au/documents/australian-jobs-publication

Bernard, R. (1994). *Research methods in anthropology: Qualitative and quantitative approaches* (2nd ed.). AltaMira Press.

Birt, L., Scott, S., Cavers, D., Campbell, C., & Walter, F. (2016). Member checking: A tool to enhance trustworthiness or merely a nod to validation? *Qualitative Health Research, 26*(13), 1802–1811.

Brookfield, S. D. (2017). *Becoming a critically reflective teacher.* John Wiley & Sons.

de Jong, T., Lazonder, A. W., Chinn, C. A., Fischer, F., Gobert, J., Hmelo-Silver, C. E., Koedinger, K. R., Krajcik, J. S., Kyza, E. A., & Linn, M. C. (2023). Let's talk evidence—The case for combining inquiry-based and direct instruction. *Educational Research Review,* 100536.

DeWalt, K., & DeWalt, B. (1998). Participant observation. In R. Bernard (Ed.), *Handbook of methods in cultural anthropology* (pp. 259–300). AltaMira Press.

Fricker, M. (2003). Epistemic justice and a role for virtue in the politics of knowing. *Metaphilosophy, 34*(1–2), 154–173.

Grainger, P., Steffler, R., de Villiers Scheepers, M., Thiele, C., & Dole, S. (2019). Student negotiated learning, student agency and general capabilities in the 21st century: The DeLorean project. *The Australian Educational Researcher, 46,* 425–447.

Hmelo-Silver, C., Golan Duncan, R., & Chinn, C. (2007). Scaffolding and achievement in problem-based and inquiry learning: A response to Kirschner, Sweller and Clark. *Educational Psychologist, 42*(2), 99–107.

Kawulich, B. (2005). Participant observation as a data collection method. *Forum: Qualitative Social Research, 6*(2) (art. 43).

Kirschner, P., Sweller, J., & Clark, R. (2006). Why minimal guidance during instruction does not work: An analysis of the failure of constructivist, discovery, problem-based, experiential, and inquiry-based teaching. *Educational Psychologist, 41*(2), 75–86.

Lazonder, A. W., & Harmsen, R. (2016). Meta-analysis of inquiry-based learning: Effects of guidance. *Review of Educational Research, 86*(3), 681–718.

Malik, Z., Khan, S., & Maqsood, M. (2018). Exploring the relationship between student engagement and new pedagogical approaches. *Journal of Educational Technology Systems, 47*(2), 170–192.

McCourt, B., & Ikutegbe, V. (2019). Supporting school completion: The importance of engagement and effective teaching. In *Learning curve issue* (Vol. 21, pp. 1–12). Centre for Education Statistics and Evaluation.

Newman, S. (2020). Teacher learning: Schön and the language of reflective practice. In *Research-informed teacher learning: Critical perspectives on theory, research and practice* (pp. 98–111). Routledge.

Renzulli, J. S. (2000). Raising the ceiling for all students: School improvement from a high-end perspective. In A. L. Costa (Ed.), *Teaching for intelligence: A collection of 11 articles* (pp. 151–77). Skylight-Hawker Brownlow.

Ritchhart, R., & Perkins, D. (2008). Making thinking visible. *Educational Leadership, 65*(5), 57.

Rossi, T., & Sirna, K. (2008). Creating physical education in remote Australian schools: Overcoming the tyranny of distance through communities of practice. *Journal of Research in Rural Education (Online), 23*(6), 1.

Schön, D. A. (1987). *Educating the reflective practitioner: Toward a new design for teaching and learning in the professions.* Jossey-Bass.

Sciacca, R. (2016). Fostering critical thinking through a critical inquiry approach in home economics. *Journal of the HEIA, 23*(2), 2–12.

Willingham, D. (2019). How to teach critical thinking. In *Education: Future frontiers.* Department of Education.

Willison, J. W. (2012). When academics integrate research skill development in the curriculum. *Higher Education Research & Development, 31*(6), 905–919.

Willison, J. (2020). *The models of engaged learning and teaching: Connecting sophisticated learning from early childhood to Ph.D.* Springer.

Willison, J., & O'Regan, K. (2007). Commonly known, commonly not known, totally unknown: A framework for students becoming researchers. *Higher Education Research and Development, 26*(4), 393–409.

Willison, J., Sabir, F., & Thomas, J. (2017). Shifting dimensions of autonomy in students' research and employment. *Higher Education Research and Development, 36*(2), 430–443.

Willison, J., Zhu, X., Xie, B., Yu, X., Chen, J., Zhang, D., Shashoug, I., & Sabir, F. (2020). Graduates' affective transfer of research skills and evidence-based practice from university to employment in clinics. *BMC Medical Education, 20*(1), 1–18.

Wilmore, M., & Willison, J. (2016). Graduates' attitudes to research skill development in undergraduate media education. *Asia Pacific Media Educator, 26*(1), 113–128.

Jason Home has been teaching for seven years, the first four of which involved primary and secondary school students in diverse subjects in a remote mining town. The last three years, Jason has been teaching his passion, Music at high school level, in a coastal school.

Tom Snelling just received his first teaching contract after casual teaching for two years during the COVID-19 Epidemic. In the research for Chapter 2, he was a preservice teacher enrolled in a Master's of Teaching degree.

John Willison is the Director of the Bachelor of Teaching at the University of Adelaide and a National Senior Teaching Fellow. He was a secondary school science teacher for 10 years using systematic approaches to improving his students learning. He has researched how teachers develop their students' research skills and other forms of sophisticated thinking for three decades.

Open Access This chapter is licensed under the terms of the Creative Commons Attribution 4.0 International License (http://creativecommons.org/licenses/by/4.0/), which permits use, sharing, adaptation, distribution and reproduction in any medium or format, as long as you give appropriate credit to the original author(s) and the source, provide a link to the Creative Commons license and indicate if changes were made.

The images or other third party material in this chapter are included in the chapter's Creative Commons license, unless indicated otherwise in a credit line to the material. If material is not included in the chapter's Creative Commons license and your intended use is not permitted by statutory regulation or exceeds the permitted use, you will need to obtain permission directly from the copyright holder.

Chapter 3
Open Educational Practices (OEPs) for Research Skill Development with In-Service School Teachers

Barbara Brown, Michele Jacobsen, Verena Roberts, Christie Hurrell, Mia Travers, and Nicole Neutzling

Abstract In this chapter, we discuss open educational practices (OEPs) that Teacher Educators (TEs) used to facilitate in-service schoolteachers' (I-STs') research thinking. The majority of graduate students in the program held teaching roles in K-12 or educational development and training roles in adult learning contexts. OEPs are participatory and collaborative learning opportunities based on social constructivist principles used in a component of a fully online Master's program in Education offered by a research university situated on the Canadian prairie. The I-STs in the program were situated as scholars of the profession and were provided with structured learning opportunities to help develop research-based skills (Brown et al. in Open Educational Practices (OEP) create conditions for learning in a graduate school, 2022; Jacobsen et al. in J Univ Teach Learn Pract 15(4):1–18, 2018). Results from our study indicate that responsive teaching is integral to OEP and can help I-STs develop research skills and research thinking.

3.1 Background

The Research Skill Development (RSD) framework (Willison & O'Regan, 2007), was used to guide the initial design and subsequent curriculum review of the Master of Education program (Jacobsen et al., 2018). RSD was used as a conceptual framework in our study to examine the ways in which open educational practices (OEPs) can be used to facilitate in-service teachers' (I-STs') research-based skill development through their examination of meaningful problems of practice in a scholarly community of inquiry. OEPs are teaching and learning approaches that promote collaborative networked learning opportunities that are digitally accessible to all learners. OEPs can include the co-creation and or use of open educational resources in digital spaces where educators and learners can reflect upon their learning in order

---

B. Brown (✉) · M. Jacobsen · V. Roberts · C. Hurrell · M. Travers · N. Neutzling
The University of Calgary, Calgary, Canada
e-mail: babrown@ucalgary.ca

to share their experiences with others (Cronin, 2017; Roberts, 2022). The six facets of RSD (Willison, 2020; Willison & O'Regan, 2007) were used as a conceptual framework to help us examine the intersections of research thinking and OEPs in a graduate program and as a lens to examine and interpret the results. We build upon the six facets of RSD to help us better understand how OEPs can be used to guide the development of research skills and research thinking for I-STs in a professional graduate program in education.

This chapter describes how the RSD Framework was used together with OEPs to purposively scaffold the development of I-ST's research skills and research thinking. It then outlines a study that involved 13 I-STs who shared their reflections on making the process and products of their research thinking explicit and accessible to a professional and academic audience that extended learning beyond the formal program. The following vignette provides an entry point into the research by describing how one of the TEs (Verena) inspired I-ST co-development of an open educational resource in the program. Further, the vignette illustrates how one of the I-STs (Nicole) benefited from the approaches used by the TEs to support her contribution to one of the pressbook volumes and how this led her to join the research team as a research assistant for the project.

3.2 Vignette: Benefits of OEP to Support Research Thinking

While the course description and learning outcomes were pre-established as part of the graduate program, Verena and TEs teaching the courses in the program worked together to determine the pedagogical approaches and how to layer the learning tasks to support I-STs in achieving the learning outcomes (Cook-Sather et al., 2014). Verena suggested extending the layered assignments in the program by adding an option for students to co-design an open educational resource (OER) (Ashton, 2017). Verena's experience and expertise in open education and the development of an Open Learning Design Framework (Roberts, 2022) also inspired the conceptualization of a research project. With a grant to support the development of a pressbook and to conduct research about student experiences, the TEs and research team worked together to incorporate OER development as part of the program for two consecutive years. After completing all of the coursework in the program, I-STs were invited to submit their final paper to be published as a chapter in an edited open pressbook (Brown et al., 2020, 2021). TEs engaged I-STs in open educational practices (OEPs), such as participatory and collaborative knowledge building activities with peers, throughout the program to create and build knowledge together that informed their own inquiry projects and development of research skills.

Nicole, one of the I-STs, reflected on the benefits of these approaches and how the use of OEPs helped her to contribute a pressbook chapter because of her work throughout the program. In her blog posts, Nicole captured her ongoing reflections during the inquiry which helped her critically evaluate information and to make decisions for next steps. In the program, Nicole's knowledge building work was scaffolded by Scardamalia and Bereiter (2010) principles of knowledge building in educational contexts. Nicole recalled how the TEs mentored and coached learners throughout the program to help form collaborative knowledge building and peer learning relationships that were guided by principles of idea improvement and community knowledge (Scardamalia & Bereiter, 2010).

Nicole connected with the TEs for timely, constructive feedback and editing support, and connected with experts outside the program (e.g., content experts, professional colleagues from their workplace, librarians and former students) to seek feedback and resources related to her topic of inquiry (Cronin & MacLaren, 2018). Connecting with a librarian and learning how to use information repositories and search engines helped Nicole and her peers find relevant resources. Connecting with a professional colleague or an expert in the topic or area of interest was also important to help Nicole recognize the relevance and interest of her inquiry for a broad audience beyond peers in the class and TEs in the program.

After the conclusion of courses, many of the I-STs like Nicole decided to share results of their inquiry publicly and submitted their paper for consideration as a chapter in one of the open pressbook volumes. Students who elected to publish their manuscript in the pressbook (9 in the 1st volume and 6 in the 2nd volume) continued to receive feedback from the TEs and members of the research team after they completed their course work in the program. With the help of an editorial review team and professional copy editor, the chapters continued to be refined by their respective authors. Nicole and many of the chapter authors returned as guest speakers in the program the following year to help inspire the next cohort of I-STs in becoming scholars of the profession and in developing their research skills. This experience with research-based learning and authentic work on an OER also led to Nicole joining the research team and becoming an advocate for increasing awareness of research-based learning and open educational practices in teacher education.

3.3 Why Integrate RSD and OEP in Masters Level Courses?

The vignette highlights some of the core ways that open educational practices—reflection, participatory and collaborative knowledge building and internal and external formative feedback—combined to facilitate research skills and research thinking. The introduction and use of the RSD Framework within the courses provided a way to both practically consider how research could be designed and scaffolded into the program and how OEPs could be used to facilitate research thinking. The RSD framework includes six facets outlining important research skills that instructors can integrate into class learning activities (Willison, 2020; Willison & O'Regan, 2007). The six facets, elaborated upon by Willison in Chap. 1

in this book outline the iterative actions and elements of research thinking. The TEs teaching courses in the program designed learning activities that aligned with the RSD facets. Griffiths (2004) noted that "processes of inquiry are highly integrated into the student learning activities" when research-based teaching occurs (p. 722). The RSD framework outlines how each facet is situated on a continuum of levels of learning autonomy and how much guidance students need from a highly structured and facilitated learning experience to a more student-led inquiry for developing research thinking.

3.4 Developmental Approach Used for Research Thinking

The TEs who taught in this program adopted Cronin's (2017) description of OEP: "collaborative practices that include the creation, use, and reuse of OER as well as pedagogical practices employing participatory technologies and social networks for interaction, peer-learning, knowledge creation, and empowerment of learners" (p. 4). The design of the program and developmental approach specifically used in four courses for developing I-STs' research thinking was guided by Cronin's description of OEP. The four courses were designed as a stand-alone graduate certificate or with the option to apply the certificate towards a Master of Education degree. It is important to note that each course included several assignments that mapped to the RSD facets and in Fig. 3.1, we illustrate how the facets mapped to the major assignments that were interconnected throughout the program using OEP and learning activities for formative assessment.

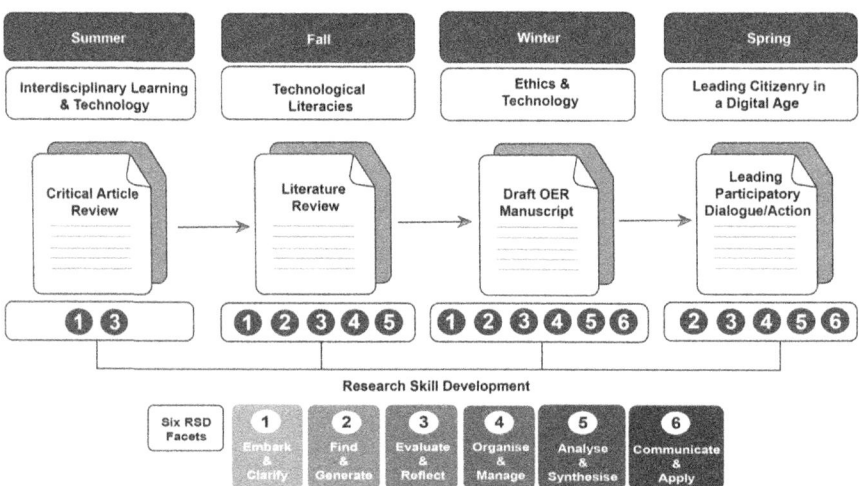

Fig. 3.1 Major assignments in four courses with alignment to RSD

In the first course during the summer term, Interdisciplinary Learning and Technology, the emphasis of the critical article review was on developing facets one: embark and clarify and three: evaluate and reflect. These facets were foundational for the subsequent assignments. Building on the skills developed during the first course, facets one through five were emphasized during the literature review assignment in the second course on Technological Literacies during the fall term. Building upon the first two courses, the third course in the winter term, Ethics and Technology, amplified all six of the facets in the major learning task (Draft OER manuscript). The fourth course in the spring term, Leading Citizenry in a Digital Age, concluded the program with an emphasis on developing facets two through six through a participatory dialogue/action-oriented assignment. Brown et al. (2022) described the progression of these key assignments across the four graduate courses in the program as layered and renewable and providing an opportunity for knowledge-building:

> Students [I-STs] had the option to remix and build on their previous work and assignments as they progressed through the four courses in the program (layered). Students [I-STs] continued to build-on and use their own openly published work during subsequent courses and beyond the duration of the program (renewable). Each of the courses provided students [I-STs] with opportunities to personalize the assignments to their professional contexts and interests (knowledge-building) (Brown et al., 2022, p. 459).

Mapping the learning tasks from the four courses to the six facets in the RSD framework helped the TEs to recognize the intersection of research skill development and OEP. For additional examples of applications of the RSD framework to postgraduate work see Heck, Chap. 4 in this book.

3.5 Co-design and Formative Assessment Strategies at the Intersection of OEP and RSD

3.5.1 Co-design

Co-design is often associated with OEP approaches and can be described as a relationship between TEs and I-STs in which the learners are positioned as active agents in the learning process and supported by their TE (Barbera et al., 2017; Jahnke et al., 2020) to complete learning tasks that are authentic and student-centered (DeRosa & Robinson, 2017). For example, I-STs selected topics for inquiry and problems of practice that emerged from their own school contexts. Co-designing and co-creating learning experiences are promising for I-STs learning and have been connected to increases in student engagement (Jacobsen et al., 2021; Paskevicius & Irvine, 2019; Wiley & Hilton, 2018). When reviewing the literature in OEP, we noted that various examples of co-design are emerging, such as building learning relationships between course participants, negotiating learning tasks, promoting student voice and choice within the course activities and course content and integrating authentic, meaningful and participatory learning activities (Barbera et al., 2017; Paskevicius & Irvine, 2019;

Roberts, 2022). However, we also noticed there is a dearth of research studying the intersections of OEP and research skill development for I-STs in online graduate education programs.

3.5.2 Formative Assessment Strategies

Formative assessment strategies *for* learning support students in deeper learning (Earl, 2012; Thomas & Brown, 2021) and diverse types of feedback can help students understand how to improve their work (William & Leahy, 2015). In the courses, TEs provided formative feedback with personalized suggestions to help I-STs to strengthen work during the course (Daly et al., 2010; Khan & Khan, 2019). Peer-feedback using assessment criteria was another common strategy facilitated by the TEs to further support I-STs with improving their work (Hegarty, 2015; William & Leahy, 2015). I-STs were continually provided with opportunities to reflect on their work and engage in self-assessments (Sutton, 2012). Other strategies involving members outside of the class, for example reaching out to experts in the field, were amplified during the final two courses of the program. During the third course, the TE invited experts in the field, including former I-STs, to provide current I-STs with feedback. In addition, the feedback process was often reflected upon in the course assignments so the TEs could track I-STs' perceptions of and appreciation of the feedback process. During the fourth course, the TE encouraged I-STs to identify experts and take the lead in reaching out to their networks for feedback. Although many of these formative feedback strategies are commonly used, it is important to note that developing feedback literacy is a skill that requires progression and sufficient time to develop trust among everyone involved in the process (Molloy et al., 2020).

3.6 Methodology

This section describes the qualitative interpretive study undertaken to investigate the intersections of research thinking and OEPs in a graduate program using the RSD as a lens to examine and interpret results. After the completion of the four courses, we recruited I-STs to be participants. Drawing on McKenney and Reeves' (2019) approach for design-based research, we aimed to develop a deeper understanding about how TEs can use OEPs (Karunanayaka & Naidu, 2017), and the ways that purposefully designed and layered assignments and formative assessment strategies can support I-STs' research skill development. For the research, the participants provided consent to share artefacts of learning, such as their blog post reflections. The study was approved by the University Research Ethics Board.

We have previously reported more detail about our study as part of our ongoing efforts to improve the design of the program (Jacobsen et al., 2018), and discussed how OEP supported the conditions for learning research-based skills (Brown et al., 2022). We recognized we needed to explore the intersection between research skill development and OEP further by examining students' reflections on their learning. In this present chapter, we draw on the reflections collected over two years from a group of 24 I-STs who were invited to participate in the study. Data included written reflections in response to open-ended survey questions completed by the I-STs (n = 13) and transcripts from interviews conducted with a subset of the survey respondents (n = 8). In the surveys and interviews, the participants were asked to reflect on their experiences during the four courses. Participants in our study who were interviewed (n = 8) also shared their blog post reflections as artefacts for analysis in the research.

For this chapter, we organized our analysis and reporting of these three types of student reflections in response to the following question:

> How do open educational practices, such as formative assessment strategies, support the conditions for learning research-based skills?

Four members of the research team analyzed the reflections using the RSD facets as the lens through which the data was interpreted. All text excerpts from the survey, interview transcripts, and blog post reflections were coded using the RSD facets and then compared across the three data sets. The results demonstrated evidence of I-STs' experiences in OEP, particularly surrounding formative assessment practices. Excerpts from students' reflections are used to help illustrate our findings in this chapter relative to the six facets of RSD and to demonstrate how responsive teaching is integral to OEP.

3.7 Results and Discussion

3.7.1 Facet 1: Embark and Clarify for Purposive Thinking

Reflections shared by the I-STs in our study demonstrated evidence of purposive thinking as they embarked on their inquiry. The following excerpt from a blog post reflection shows how one I-ST noted the importance of recognizing the influences that background experiences and contexts can have when embarking on an inquiry and how the opportunity to reflect on these experiences can inform the purpose of the inquiry:

> I have blogged weekly (or more) about the course readings and my reflections on the world as it relates to the course. Each week, I tried to relate what I read in the assigned readings to my own context as an [I-ST] or as a learner myself. I have recognized that my personal context has shaped my perception of education and the ethical issues associated with educational technology. I've already acknowledged that I have a significant amount of privilege when it comes to education, but my age and educational experiences also shape my perceptions.

In this excerpt, this I-ST acknowledged how their workplace setting influenced thinking about their topic of inquiry related to ethical issues of educational technology. This connection between context and inquiry was a common sentiment expressed by the I-STs when describing what led them to selecting their topic of inquiry and determining there was a need to explore the topic. As one way to embark on the inquiry, I-STs shared their topic of inquiry with the TEs, their peers, and with external audiences. The TEs used OEPs, such as an elevator pitch, to provide opportunities for I-STs to test out their inquiry idea with peers. This is an example of responsive teaching as an OEP that can be used to help support I-STs as they are developing research-based skills and beginning the process of identifying their topic of inquiry by engaging openly with peers. I-STs developed purposive thinking as they worked out what they wanted to do, and what was meaningful for their learning and teaching situation when they clarified the purpose of their inquiry. When implementing responsive teaching as an OEP, the TEs empowered I-STs to take an active role in their own learning journey (Barbera et al., 2017; Jahnke et al., 2020).

3.7.2 Facet 2: Find and Generate for Informed Thinking

The development of an open education resource required I-STs to find and generate information for their inquiry and was a result of student work accomplished throughout the courses, including the development of a draft manuscript in the third course. One of the survey respondents described the process as a collective product that resulted from co-design:

> In this case, collaboration (co-labour) directly describes the idea that the end product, the OER chapter, is actually a product of many minds and many hands. Students are traditionally restricted to their own abilities and the resources they find independently. Co-design utilizes an ongoing feedback loop where the opinions, suggestions, and resources from others are valued.

TEs used responsive teaching as an OEP to help students find information to help prepare a manuscript for publication in an open pressbook. I-STs also helped each other by sharing resources (DiPietro, 2013). For example, one of the layered learning activities involved using Twitter and a common hashtag (#EdTechEthics) to help students curate resources (Brown & Roberts, 2023). One of the I-STs blog post reflections captures how this learner used this approach to share resources:

> I've found that having the #EdTechEthics hashtag has allowed me to connect with classmates and faculty in a different way. When stumbling across an article or source that might be applicable to others, it's a simple link shared on Twitter to the entire group following the hashtag and/or a direct tag to a classmate to alert them to a possible source for their research. This casual browsing of information is much more conducive to my learning style, allowing me time to process and browse to find things of interest without feeling the need to respond.

This excerpt demonstrates how an I-ST viewed the use of the Twitter feed as a worthwhile strategy for identifying relevant sources. Another I-STs survey response described how the learning activities in the courses offered an ongoing opportunity to find and access information from a broader network of supports:

The course was not conducted in isolation. The integration of Twitter and the publicly accessible blogs made the learning open to the world and therefore more authentic. The utilization of the wider #edtechethics community brought the possibility of engaging with others around the world who have been working on the topics and provided the opportunity to expand the student's professional learning network.

The I-STs continued to use the Twitter feed throughout their inquiry to find information and share information with peers and as noted by one interview participant, "it felt like a community project." I-STs used informed thinking to review information curated through the common hashtag and to find relevant information for their inquiry. When implementing responsive teaching as an OEP, the TEs engaged I-STs in providing mutual assistance and acknowledged the significance of peer input and open resource sharing (Di Pietro, 2013; Hegarty, 2015; William & Leahy, 2015). For additional examples of integrating social media in learning activities and RSD, see Mataniari et al., Chap. 6 in this book.

3.7.3 Facet 3: Evaluate and Reflect for Astute Thinking

This open access to shared resources also required I-STs to discern the credibility of sources, referred to as astute thinking when evaluating and reflecting. The following I-ST described using this strategy to expand their professional learning network

> This platform is most challenging for me, as it is so open – that being both its strength and a potential point of concern for me....I rarely used Twitter but now I see the potential that all the academics raved about. It is informative, to the point, so I have actually been following a few authors that I have read while writing a chapter .... I really found Twitter to be cool and energetic and glad to be connected to such knowledgeable perspectives and minds. In fact, I think I may go back to our hashtag and see if there are any more "edtech" people out there for me to follow (Blog Post Reflection).

When TEs were using responsive teaching as an OEP, I-STs were developing research skills and learning how to provide and receive feedback in formal (e.g., course learning management system) and informal learning spaces (e.g., blog spaces) for reflection (Earl, 2012). The sheer amount of feedback provided from different sources presented a challenge for many I-STs; nevertheless, the students appreciated the constructive feedback as described by one of the blog post reflections:

> I was able to use their [externals] feedback, as well as the feedback of my group to strengthen my chapter significantly. My groupmates all came from different professional contexts and we were exploring vastly different topics, however I found that we were all able to give each other helpful feedback and provide ideas that others hadn't thought about ... has caused me to rethink many of my previously held opinions. It has caused me to consider what ethical behavior looks like in relation to the use of technology, both in education and beyond.

As a demonstration of the third facet of RSD (evaluate and reflect), the I-STs required astute thinking for reviewing formative feedback and when making decisions about using or not using the feedback provided. The TEs established instructional frameworks that enabled students to effectively discern and act upon feedback (William & Leahy, 2015) when implementing responsive teaching as an OEP.

3.7.4 Facet 4: Organise and Manage for Harmonised Thinking

In their reflections the participants shared how some of the feedback provided, particularly that from their peers, was not always useful and that students preferred specific feedback with concrete suggestions on how to make the improvements instead of broader recommendations that could move the inquiry into a completely different direction. As we reviewed the reflections, we noted the I-STs benefited from and felt challenged by the feedback process with their TEs and peers. In relationship to organise and manage, one of the interview respondents said, "It was nice to bounce ideas off of people who were in the same situation and had the same understanding of what was expected of us, even if we started off a little bit confused." Similarly, one of the survey respondents commented that peer feedback was helpful when managing so much information, "It was a great way to push me and develop skills I was weak on." I-STs also reflected on the comfort and level of trust in sharing work with peers who they previously worked with and "if you're just throwing your work out into a random stranger's eyes, it can be a little bit nerve-racking, so it's a bit easier if you know you trust the people." In a blog post reflection, one of the I-STs recognized the value in reviewing work created by peers and learning about different ways to organise and manage information using shared documents (e.g., google docs):

> Our group shared our diagrams/outlines with one another and found that all of us are quite different in how we process our information, not a surprising fact but I find it simply interesting to see how others brainstorm and organise their thoughts. Not to mention how fascinating the various topics are. I appreciate the feedback and knowledge they can provide when sharing their own experiences.

Responsive teaching involves making provisions for formative feedback opportunities to help I-STs organise their ideas and harmonise thinking about their inquiry. When implementing responsive teaching as an OEP, the TEs incorporated mechanisms that facilitated continuous feedback regarding both the process and outcomes of the inquiry (Molloy et al., 2020; Thomas & Brown, 2021).

3.7.5 Facet 5: Analyze and Synthesise for Insightful Thinking

Formative feedback also helped I-STs develop insightful thinking as they developed a synthesis and understanding of their inquiry. One of the interview participants described formative feedback for purposes of synthesis: "It's like a piece of art. You just keep adding to it, molding it constantly to get this one final artifact." Another interview participant described this aspect of the inquiry as an "opportunity to hone research skills and writing, analysis, assessment, what to include, what not to include, how to relate your particular chapter to personal experience." In a blog post reflection, one of the I-STs reflected on the value of receiving input from peers to help understand what ideas needed more elaboration to clarify how the information was synthesised:

> [With] suggestions to use headings, I pulled apart what I wrote, started a new document, and put my ideas down in an organised manner. As it turns out, even at that point, I had a lot of the main ideas, I just needed to support it and explore it more.

Developing feedback literacy is a skill that requires a progression and sufficient time to develop trust among everyone involved in the process (Molloy et al., 2020). One of the limitations of our study is that we conducted the research immediately following the completion of the four courses; however, the I-STs development of the OER chapter continued for many months after the completion of the courses. Additional feedback was provided to students from external sources, such as an editorial team and professional copy editor. When implementing responsive teaching as an OEP, the TEs promoted I-STs feedback literacy via the acquisition and use of feedback from external sources (William & Leahy, 2015).

3.7.6 Facet 6: Communicate and Apply for Externalised Thinking

It is possible, if we collected data again after the publication of the OER, that reflections would have illustrated externalised thinking and the ways I-STs applied their understanding to their professional practice. The following excerpt from one of the blog post reflections shows how one I-ST reflected on their journey through the research process when developing the draft OER manuscript:

> I really pushed myself in my research. This is the first time I have recorded all the articles, websites, blogs, etc., that I looked at to gain information about [inquiry] in the classroom. I used a spreadsheet to organise the information. I also tapped into the expertise of the university librarians....and Twitter....see my post about ....The feedback that was given to me. I was able to get support from my classmates and instructor, as well as my colleagues and friends. They all contributed valuable and diverse perspectives that caused me to reflect and reshape my thinking.

During the interviews, one of the I-STs reflected, "I feel I had the opportunity to gain applicable skills that I can apply in the classroom." For example, one I-ST described how reflective blogging could be used in the classroom, which is promising evidence of the potential for transfer to professional work. When implementing responsive teaching as an OEP, the TEs demonstrated a strong presence and attentiveness in providing constructive feedback that can translate into further practice (Daly et al., 2010; Khan & Khan, 2019; William & Leahy, 2015).

In the future, we recommend conducting another round of data collection later, so that participants have an opportunity to comment on externalised thinking and ways the inquiry may have informed their teaching. We still wonder if the I-STs perceptions of the feedback changed after the completion and publication of the OER chapter. For example, how did the I-STs perceptions about the amount of feedback, or type of peer feedback, or outside expert feedback change after their work was published? How did the I-STs experiences with OEPs and OER impact their professional practice? In the data we also noted feedback provided by the TEs was viewed as supportive and responsive for meeting their learning needs; however, there was less discussion about students' self-reflections. Did I-STs' perceptions about self-reflections or creating blog post reflections change in any way after their OER chapter was published? Further research is needed to continue exploring the RSD facets and thinking developed during the program and following the program when TEs used OEPs and some of the I-STs collaboratively contributed to an OER.

3.8 Conclusion

Our research team's contribution is unique as it describes how TEs interweaved research skill development with open educational practices to scaffold I-STs research thinking. Each course was designed with layered and renewable assignments, and formative feedback strategies, to engage I-STs in research thinking. RSD was a helpful framework to inform TEs learning design of participatory and collaborative knowledge building tasks to explicitly engage facets of research thinking, such as embark and clarify, find, and generate, and evaluate and reflect. This design, along with our research approach using RSD as a lens to examine and interpret results, made the outcomes of I-STs inquiry projects and evidence of research thinking explicit and accessible to a broader professional and academic audience beyond the duration of a program. Intentional reflection on inquiry processes via regular blog post reflections and feedback from the TEs and others supported I-STs in self-identification as researchers who developed and enacted diverse research skills that amplified facets of research thinking. Analysis and reporting on three types of student reflections using the RSD as a lens provided evidence of I-STs' research skill and research thinking relative to the six facets of RSD.

By providing the invitation to present, reflect, and blog openly about their inquiry projects, many I-STs were able to gain insights about their research experiences and processes, and to enhance their knowledge building through peer support, and collaborative peer feedback. The participatory and collaborative activities demonstrate responsive teaching, which is integral to OEP, helped students to engage in an inquiry, develop research skills, and employ research thinking. Our research on the intersection of open educational practices and research thinking demonstrates the value of RSD as both a design strategy and as a lens for interpreting research results. Using open educational practices in a graduate program is a promising learning approach for research skill development with in-service schoolteachers.

References

Ashton, H. (Ed.). (2017). *Structuring equality: A handbook for student-centered learning and teaching practices*. The Graduate Centre Learning Collective. https://www.hastac.org/collections/structuring-equality-handbook-student-centered-learning-and-teaching-practices

Barbera, E., Garcia, I., & Fuertes-Alpiste, M. (2017). A co-design process microanalysis: Stages and facilitators of an inquiry-based and technology-enhanced learning scenario. *International Review of Research in Open and Distributed Learning, 18*(6), 104–126.

Brown, B., Jacobsen, M., Roberts, V., Hurrell, C., Neutzling, N., & Travers-Hayward, M. (2022). Open Educational Practices (OEP) create conditions for learning in a graduate school. In M. Jacobsen, & C. Smith (Eds.), *Online learning and teaching from kindergarten to graduate school* (pp. 457–483). Canadian Association for Teacher Education. https://doi.org/10.11575/PRISM/40509

Brown, B., & Roberts, V. (2023). Using Twitter for online learning: #EdTechEthics, a course that never ends…. In M. Arcellana-Panlilio, & P. Dyjur (Eds.), *Fostering student success in online learning* (pp. 14–18). Taylor Institute for Teaching and Learning Guide Series. https://taylorinstitute.ucalgary.ca/resources/fostering-student-success-guide

Brown, B., Roberts, V., Jacobsen, M., & Hurrell, C. (Eds.). (2020). *Ethical use of technology in digital learning environments: Graduate student perspectives* (Vol. 1). University of Calgary. https://doi.org/10.11575/ant1-kb38

Brown, B., Roberts, V., Jacobsen, M., & Hurrell, C. (Eds.). (2021). *Ethical use of technology in digital learning environments: Graduate student perspectives* (Vol. 2). University of Calgary. https://doi.org/10.11575/PRISM/39490

Cook-Sather, A., Bovill, C., Felten, P., & Cook, M. (2014). *Engaging students as partners in learning and teaching: A guide for faculty*. The Jossey-Bass Higher and Adult Education Series.

Cronin, C. (2017). Openness and praxis: Exploring the use of open educational practices in higher education. *The International Review of Research in Open and Distributed Learning, 18*(5), 1–21. https://doi.org/10.19173/irrodl.v18i5.3096

Cronin, C., & MacLaren, I. (2018). Conceptualising OEP: A review of theoretical and empirical literature in Open Educational Practices. *Open Praxis, 10*(2), 127. https://doi.org/10.5944/openpraxis.10.2.825

Daly, C., Pachler, N., Mor, Y., & Mellar, H. (2010). Exploring formative e-assessment: Using case stories and design patterns. *Assessment and Evaluation in Higher Education, 35*(5), 619–636. https://doi.org/10.1080/02602931003650052

DeRosa, R., & Robison, S. (2017). From OER to open pedagogy: Harnessing the power of open. In R. Jhangiani, & R. Biswas-Diener (Eds.), *Open*. Ubiquity Press. https://doi.org/10.5334/bbc.i

DiPietro, P. (2013). Transforming education with new media: Participatory pedagogy, interactive learning and Web 2.0. *The International Journal of Technology, Knowledge, and Society, 8*(5), 1–11. https://doi.org/10.18848/1832-3669/CGP/v08i05/56321

Earl, L. (2012). *Assessment as learning: Using classroom assessment to maximize student learning* (2nd ed.). Corwin.

Griffiths, R. (2004). Knowledge production and the research-teaching nexus: The case of the built environment disciplines. *Studies in Higher Education, 29*(6), 709–726. https://doi.org/10.1080/0307507042000287212

Hegarty, B. (2015). Attributes of open pedagogy: A model for using open educational resources. *Educational Technology, 55*(4), 3–13. https://www.jstor.org/stable/44430383

Jacobsen, M., Brown, B., Roberts, V., Hurrell, C., Neutzling, N., & Travers-Howard, M. (2021). Open learning designs and participatory pedagogies for graduate student online publishing. In *Proceedings of the teaching culturally and linguistically diverse international students in open and/or online learning environments: A research symposium* (pp. 1–8). University of Windsor. https://scholar.uwindsor.ca/itos21/session3/session3/9/

Jacobsen, M., McDermott, M., Brown, B., Eaton, S., & Simmons, M. (2018). Graduate students' research-based learning experiences in an online Master of Education program. *Journal of University Teaching and Learning Practice, 15*(4), 1–18. https://doi.org/10.53761/1.15.4.4

Jahnke, I., Meinke-Kroll, M., Todd, M., & Nolte, A. (2020). Exploring artifact-generated learning with digital technologies: Advancing active learning with co-design in higher education across disciplines. *Technology, Knowledge and Learning.* https://doi.org/10.1007/s10758-020-09473-3

Karunanayaka, S. P., & Naidu, S. (2017). A design-based approach to support and nurture open educational practices. *Asian Association of Open Universities Journal, 12*(1), 1–20. https://doi.org/10.1108/AAOUJ-01-2017-0010

Khan, S., & Khan, R. A. (2019). Online assessments: Exploring perspectives of university students. *Education and Information Technologies, 24*(1), 661–667. https://doi.org/10.1007/s10639-018-9797-0

Molloy, E., Boud, D., & Henderson, M. (2020). Developing a learning-centred framework for feedback literacy. *Assessment and Evaluation in Higher Education, 45*(4), 527–540. https://doi.org/10.1080/02602938.2019.1667955

McKenney, S., & Reeves, T. C. (2019). *Conducting educational research* (2nd ed.). Routledge.

Paskevicius, M., & Irvine, V. (2019). Open education and learning design: Open pedagogy in praxis. *Journal of Interactive Media in Education, 2019*(1), 1–10. https://doi.org/10.5334/jime.512

Roberts, V. (2022). Open learning design for using open educational practices in high school learning contexts and beyond. *Journal for Multicultural Education, 16*(5), 491–507. https://doi.org/10.1108/JME-01-2022-0019

Scardamalia, M., & Bereiter, C. (2010). A brief history of knowledge building. *Canadian Journal of Learning and Technology, 36*(1), 1–6. https://doi.org/10.21432/T2859M

Sutton, P. (2012). Conceptualizing feedback literacy: Knowing, being, and acting. *Innovations in Education and Teaching International, 49*(1), 31–40. https://doi.org/10.1080/14703297.2012.647781

Thomas, C., & Brown, B. (2021). Formative assessment strategies for group work. *Education in the North, 28*(2), 134–155. https://doi.org/10.26203/z6ab-rm62

Wiley, D., & Hilton III, J. L. (2018). Defining OER-enabled pedagogy. *International Review of Research in Open and Distributed Learning, 19*(4). https://doi.org/10.19173/irrodl.v19i4.3601

William, D., & Leahy, S. (2015). *Embedding formative assessment.* Learning Sciences International.

Willison, J. (2020). *The models of engaged learning and teaching: Connecting sophisticated learning from early childhood to Ph.D.* Springer.

Willison, J., & O'Regan, K. (2007). Commonly known, commonly not known, totally unknown: A framework for students becoming researchers. *Higher Education Research and Development, 26*(4), 393–409. https://doi.org/10.1080/07294360701658609

Barbara Brown is an Associate Professor, Associate Dean, Teaching and Learning in the Werklund School of Education and Academic Coordinator for the *Leading and Learning in a Digital Age* stackable certificate in the M.Ed. Interdisciplinary Program. Her research interests include research-practice partnerships, professional learning, and instructional design in digital learning environments.

Michele Jacobsen is a Professor in the Learning Sciences in the Werklund School of Education at the University of Calgary. Her research is focused on learning and participatory pedagogies in technology enabled learning environments, online faculty development, science and technology communication, and learning designs to sponsor knowledge building and intellectual engagement.

Verena Roberts is an Adjunct Assistant Professor with the Werklund School of Education at the University of Calgary. Her research interests include learning design, open learning, open educational resources (OER) and pedagogy (OEP), participatory learning and high school redesign.

Christie Hurrell is the Director, Lab NEXT in Libraries and Cultural Resources at the University of Calgary. Her role involves advancing digital research initiatives and partnerships, working on scholarly communication and open education initiatives, and coordinating Lab NEXT, the library's digital scholarship collaboration space and makerspace.

Mia Travers is a Research Assistant with the Werklund School of Education at the University of Calgary. Her research interests include open and digital learning, decolonizing schooling, and inequalities in education.

Nicole Neutzling is a graduate student at the Werklund School of Education at the University of Calgary. Her past coursework has focused on educational neuroscience and leading and learning in the digital age. Nicole is an OER Research Fellow and interested in the use and perceptions of OER and OEP at the K-12 level.

Open Access This chapter is licensed under the terms of the Creative Commons Attribution 4.0 International License (http://creativecommons.org/licenses/by/4.0/), which permits use, sharing, adaptation, distribution and reproduction in any medium or format, as long as you give appropriate credit to the original author(s) and the source, provide a link to the Creative Commons license and indicate if changes were made.

The images or other third party material in this chapter are included in the chapter's Creative Commons license, unless indicated otherwise in a credit line to the material. If material is not included in the chapter's Creative Commons license and your intended use is not permitted by statutory regulation or exceeds the permitted use, you will need to obtain permission directly from the copyright holder.

Chapter 4
Exploring In-Service Teacher-Researcher Reflexivity: Education Research as Cultural Work

Deborah Heck

Abstract This chapter explores the evidence within In-Service teachers' (I-STs) (n = 8) publications of their use of the Research Skills Development (RSD) framework as they research and then write about a contemporary educational issue relevant to their educational practice in Australia. The practising I-STs were completing their first semester of a Master of Education program in a course that used the RSD framework. The analysis of the published work of the enrolled I-STs, conducted by a Teacher Educator (TE) identified I-ST reflexivity at the commencement of a postgraduate program of study to understand the value of the RSD framework to support I-ST empowerment as researchers of classroom practice. The implications of this work provide scope for researchers and practitioners to engage in dialogue that counters the sole focus on a technical 'what works' view of educational research and opens the potential for I-STs to engage with the cultural role of research to produce new ways to recognise the complexity of the relationship between educational research, practice and thinking in classrooms—to become responsive teachers.

4.1 Background

In-service teachers (I-STs) engaging in postgraduate studies as part of mid-career professional development enter their studies with various views of educational research. Typically, they see themselves as readers and users of research. In the context of Australia, there has been a significant shift toward a reliance by policymakers on a "what works" agenda. An emphasis from policymakers to fund large-scale meta-analysis studies that translate research into specific classroom implementation strategies has resulted in funding for research being funnelled into establishing independent bodies to translate research into measurable classroom practices. The Australian Education Research Organisation (AERO) is a recent example of an organisation established to undertake this work. The organisation aims to generate

---

D. Heck (✉)
University of the Sunshine Coast, Sippy Downs, Australia
e-mail: dheck@usc.edu.au

© The Author(s) 2024
J. Willison (ed.), *Research Thinking for Responsive Teaching*,
SpringerBriefs in Education, https://doi.org/10.1007/978-981-99-6679-0_4

and present to practitioners and policymakers evidence for implementation. The standards of evidence chosen guide the focus on a narrow interpretation of what constitutes research evidence and emphasise the technical role of research. While there is an acknowledgment of the need for teacher reflection, AERO's reflection guide begins with the narrow research base identified rather than including the practitioner's evidence (Australian Education Research Organisation, 2021). Hence, there is no evidence of space for the cultural role of research and practitioner knowledge. This chapter explores the evidence of applying the Research Skills Development (RSD) framework (Willison & O'Regan, 2007) within the publications of I-STs (n = 8) at an Australian regional university. The analysis of the published work of the enrolled I-STs identified their reflexivity at the commencement of a postgraduate program of study to understand the value of the RSD framework to support I-ST empowerment as researchers of classroom practice. As a Teacher Educator (TE), I start with a vignette to bring to life my context, practice, and engagement with I-STs and the RSD Framework and the opportunity for responsive teaching to emerge.

4.2 Vignette: Master's Zoom Class

What a difference a semester makes in the life of an I-ST undertaking a postgraduate Master of Education. As I joined my online zoom class for the beginning of semester 2, I found the group discussing publication progress, sharing links and congratulating each other on recent acceptances of published work, and discussing ways to engage with publishers or readers. This scene is a stark contrast to the beginning of semester 1 when the group of I-STs commenced their study. The group are now reflecting on how their initial narrow view of the connection between teaching, practice and research in education expanded as the semester progressed. It is wonderful to take a moment to see the exhilaration and joy as these I-STs engage in these deep and respectful discussions providing support to one another and reflecting on how their engagement and contribution to education discussions make a difference. I have been drawn to the work of Santoro (2019), who challenges the contemporary emphasis in the media on teachers leaving or not being attracted to the profession because they are burnt out. She counters this argument with the view that these teachers are not so much burnt out as frustrated and disillusioned with contemporary education policy and practices. The I-STs in my zoom classroom are the anthesis of these images. They are basking in the exhilaration of engaging in something challenging, staying with it and then sharing their new knowledge with those who might be able to do something about it on Monday. The emphasis in the course is on returning many teachers to why they joined the profession in the first place and their concerns about social justice and making a difference in the lives of young people. We explored the purposes of education (Biesta, 2015) and engaged with the opportunity to explore an educational issue that "focuses on the value of education as part of what it is to live a good life" (Griffiths, 2012, p. 655). The two initial cohorts completing this semester 1 course had expanded their horizons, examined their world and work from different perspectives and often ended up in places that none of us imagined when the semester began.

4.3 Why RSD in Postgraduate Study

Most I-STs returning to study at the postgraduate level are familiar with undergraduate education that require students to engage with specific readings and complete a range of short-term tasks and assessments on a wide range of topics for each course. The shift in postgraduate level education courses to selecting your area of interest and engaging in a sustained investigation on one topic across various assessment tasks is somewhat unfamiliar. The RSD framework offered a lens to consider the key facets that the course should cover identifying the topic, different ways to find information, developing ways to be reflexive about what and how that information is found, managing the volume of information available on a topic, redefining the topic as understandings emerge, finding a range of different viewpoints synthesising, analysing and evaluating. The RSD facets (Willison, 2018) were helpful as the course learning outcomes and the assessment was designed. Table 4.1 illustrates how course learning outcomes and RSD facets align. The three assessment tasks, explained further in Sect. 4.5, were designed to support my work as a TE to continually divert I-ST attention back to the world and their topic of interest as a means to engage with responsive teaching.

The developmental focus of the RSD's levels of autonomy across the range from supervisor prescribed research to unbounded research provided in the format of a rubric was counter to my own understanding and experiences of research as cyclic and, at times, two steps forward and three steps back. The levels of autonomy did not help assist me in diverting I-STs attention back to consider what the world they live in might be asking of them as they explored their topic. This aligns with Biesta's

Table 4.1 RSD embedded in course learning outcomes

Course learning outcome	RSD facet (Willison, 2018)
1. Select and justify an issue or problem in contemporary education practice that contributes to social justice and/or sustainability	Embark and clarify Find and generate
2. Identify and critically analyse the rigour of published research related to the contemporary issue or problem	Find and generate Evaluate and reflect
3. Investigate and evaluate education practice using advanced theories, concepts and standpoints	Organise and manage Analyse and synthelsle
4. Apply reflexivity in education research	Find and generate Evaluate and reflect Analyse and synthesise
5. Generate communication using academic integrity to impact education practice and policy	Communicate and apply

(2017) concern about how temporal developmental scales generate a linear view of education. Hence, my focus is on the facets and their descriptions rather than the levels of autonomy (see McLeod Chap. 7 for a detailed use of levels of autonomy). The RSD framework was embedded in the course structure, and approach only shared in full later in the course when the I-ST had more of an understanding of the cyclic rather than linear nature of education research as part of my own responsive teaching pedagogy. For additional examples of applications of RSD frameworks in the context of postgraduate study see Brown et al., Chap. 3 in this book.

4.4 Theoretical Framing of Research Thinking

As a university TE working in higher education, one of the challenges I face in my work is considering how postgraduate study by I-STs achieves the purposes of education. It is useful to be guided in my work by the work of Biesta (2017) who suggests that we need to take up the role of teacher and consider both what should be learned and the reason for the learning. Reframing teaching in this way identifies the UE's central role and rejects the contemporary focus on learners as objects and educational time as linear and developmental. Reframing teaching in this way has also changed my orientation to practice and allowed me to explore the three purposes of education in the first-semester course. Biesta (2020b) suggests the key functions of education include qualifications, socialisation, and subjectification. *Qualifications* are focussed on knowledge and skills about how the world works, and *socialisation* examines how cultural practices and traditions influence the (re)presented knowledge and skills. The third function, *subjectification,* explains the way education restricts or enhances students as individuals. As I wrote the course, I considered carefully how the course might be an opportunity for I-STs to encounter the world and education research and the breadth of the functions of education. Postgraduate I-STs engage in a Master of Education to achieve a qualification they can add to their curriculum vitae. However, I was interested in reflecting on the possibilities of engaging with the course, with me as a teacher and the collective group of I-STs. There could be space for deep engagement with research thinking and even for the possibilities of the socialisation and subjectification functions of education to be encountered. Can teachers in this in-service Master's in Education context engage more publicly as intellectuals in their work? (Heck, 2022).

Subjectification was the most challenging of these three aspects to consider as the UE. Can I create a context where postgraduate I-STs have the freedom to deeply consider something they are curious about in the world of education? Biesta (2022, p. 91) recently summed up the idea that students might ask, "what the world is asking from me?" When designing this course in 2019, I considered this question by reflecting on my own professional trajectory and the way I had not imagined where I would end up and what I would be doing in the world as a teacher. I reflected on what I might have needed from my TE that would allow me to engage in the world in ways I could not imagine? I now realise I was considering the notion of providing an opportunity for I-STs to ask what the world is asking of them as an educator. An opportunity for I-ST to explore what it means to engage with research as a core part of their work. Teachers who engage with research as part of their postgraduate study have confidence in their research literacy and ability to make critical judgements and decisions as professionals (Woore et al., 2020). What emerges is a different view of professionalism based on the expertise of teacher judgements that I feel underpins responsive teaching.

The challenge as a TE comes as I navigate the disjuncture between my views of education research and teacher professionalism with contemporary policy and practice. The world of schools and teaching has become increasingly focused on a quality and effectiveness agenda privileging research that uses randomised controlled trials. This "what works" agenda has been criticised for bypassing teachers as professionals, at a time when policymakers adopt evidence from selected research for implementation in schools (Krejsler, 2017). My role as the TE is to continue taking up the challenge from Biesta (2022) to be the teacher who re-directs and refocuses the I-STs attention back to their topic and what the world might be asking of them. This included problematising the "what works" agenda and identifying the need to focus more on how we might go about teaching students (Siegel & Biesta, 2021). Hence, it is helpful to consider research in terms of how it might be used or provide meaning for educational practice. Biesta (2016) suggests that research can undertake both a technical and cultural role. Most I-STs are familiar with education research's technical role in generating knowledge for educational practice. However, educational research's cultural role in making sense of the world in different ways is a very new concept. Exploring the cultural role means embracing the lack of clarity offered by research as an opportunity to explore different ways to engage with and understand educational practices that underpin responsive teaching.

I grappled with how I would work as a TE to redirect attention to different ways of thinking about education research and considered providing a focus for I-STs that connects back to the core values that drew them to the profession contributing to human good through either social justice or sustainability lens. My re-direction role was taking shape in the form of researcher reflexivity. I found it helpful to consider how I could work with I-STs to understand how their perspectives changed over time (Gerstl-Pepin & Patrizio, 2009). My ongoing work as a TE is to continue the dialogue in the classroom by engaging in questions and redirecting, which underpins my own practice as a responsive teacher. My redirection is often framed by the three considerations suggested by Biesta (2020a), reminding us to consider that education is not certain and continues to be an experiment, that education does have a purpose, and is not focussed only on producing objects but also contributing to human good.

4.5 Making the Shift to Postgraduate Research

Designing assessment tasks is a requirement for the qualifications component of education to meet university accreditation requirements. Another challenge was the multiple aspects of the university systems that return us as educators to a linear notion of time and a developmental notion of learning, including such rudimentary notions as specified start and finish dates and assessment submission deadlines. A nested assessment design was generated to allow I-STs to cycle back and revisit their research thinking. The final task as a draft publication was generated so that I-STs could review the feedback and then take the work into the world beyond the bounds of the course. An overview of the formative and summative aspects of the three assessment tasks and their connection to the RSD framework provide the context for analysing the final submitted publications analysed in this chapter.

Task 1 focussed on each I-ST thinking about a topic connected to social justice or sustainability in their practice. A formative first assessment item allowed all in the group to discuss and collectively refine the topics for investigation. At this stage of the semester, the work was focused on embarking and clarifying the issues to be investigated, finding information, deciding what would be useful and then managing the arrangement of often a large volume of material. Many I-STs began with a big idea and developed their understandings of a specific topic based on their practice, reading from academic literature, professional readings, policy, and curriculum documents. The summative assessment item for this task was a written description of the contemporary issue and an explanation of the reflexive process used to identify this topic and how the topic connected to social justice or sustainability and education theory.

Task 2 invited I-STs to explore the breadth of research available via university library databases that are often not accessible to I-STs. Building on the work in task 1, I-STs then examine the different types of scholarship and explore additional ways to find, analyse, evaluate, and assess educational research. An annotated bibliography format was selected for this task because it allowed for ongoing and continual refinement of the assessment piece facilitating an iterative rather than a sequential approach. The shift here was to enable I-STs to continue finding and removing items from the annotated list and replacing them quickly. The assessment task was also concerned with developing ways to manage, organise, and evaluate ideas as a researcher when deeply examining a topic. Unlike much undergraduate study, I-STs in this context needed to understand the importance of revisiting and rereading research as a crucial aspect of being a reflexive researcher. The task provided an opportunity for I-ST to rearticulate their refined understanding of the educational issue or topic and how it connected with social justice or sustainability before selecting ten research papers to create an annotated bibliography and another opportunity to define the contemporary issue and its relevance to social justice or sustainability in education.

Task 3 invites I-STs to share their new understandings with an appropriate audience. The professional writing portfolio asked I-STs to consider an audience, a message, and a public way to engage and share their message in the form of a lead or feature article in a professional journal or magazine. The portfolio included both the manuscript and a detailed description of the choice of journal and audience for the message. The published work of the I-STs forms the data set for analysis of the RSD framework in this chapter.

4.6 Methodology

A qualitative interpretive research design was adopted in this study to explore how the facets of the RSD were evidenced in I-ST professional scholarship. The published work of the 2020 and 2021 I-STs undertaking the Researching Education course was analysed to identify the ways each facet of the RSD was evidenced in the nine published papers. A total of 18 IS-Ts participated in two-course offerings in the first semester of 2020 and 2021, nine I-STs each year. In 2020, 2 I-STs achieved three publications, while in 2021, six I-STs published their work. The nine published papers form the data set for analysis of how the published work evidenced the RSD Framework.

The study generated narrative descriptions of how the I-STs used the six facets of the RSD Framework (Willison & O'Regan, 2018) in their publications. This analysis was achieved through the application of Miles et al. (2020) first and second cycle coding to describe how the publications evidenced I-STs reference or use of the RSD facets. First cycle coding involved identifying the key topics evidenced in the text based on the RSD facets. While the second cycle coding drew together the pattern evidenced across the publications in the form of a narrative description of each RSD facet using evidence from the data to support the emerging patterns and themes identified.

4.7 Results and Discussion: Researcher Skills in I-ST Publications

The findings and discussion illuminate the evidence of the six facets of the RSD framework using examples from the I-ST publications. I begin with communicating and applying because the data analysed are the published work of the first two cohorts completing the Researching Education course. It is essential to note the iterative, cyclical and overlapping nature of the facets that can be lost in their sequential presentations as findings.

4.7.1 Communicate and Apply

The nine published papers developed by the cohort of 18 I-STs, who completed the course of study, evidence these teachers' ability to communicate and apply research that concerns them as classroom teachers. It is helpful to begin with this aspect of research skill development because the papers generated by I-STs form the data set used in this study. These papers represent each I-ST's ability to communicate with a particular audience about an educational issue or problem. Two groups of issues or problems were the focus of inquiry and publication by the cohort. The first was curriculum and pedagogy, including topics such as access and use of information and communication technology in schools (Cochrane, 2020), mathematics anxiety and pedagogy (Anson, 2021), special education curriculum (Burke, 2021) and student engagement with nature (Poeder, 2021). The second group of topics were focused on teacher wellbeing and support. These contributions examined topics such as teacher resilience and self-efficacy (Greensill, 2020a; Smith, 2021), teacher job satisfaction and work-life balance (Greensill, 2020b; Miller, 2021) and the development of teacher induction programs for alternative school contexts (Andrews, 2021).

There were submissions to three categories of publication: professional association journals, online not for profit newsletters and online commercial publisher newsletters or journals. Each author identified and aligned their message with the audience, the publication aims and their key messages. All publication options did not require authors to pay fees or charges to publish their work. Three of the publications were submitted to professional associations journals. For example: the Association of Heads of Independent Schools of Australia publishes the journal Independence (Andrews, 2021). The Australian Association of Mathematics Teachers launched in 2019 a new journal Australian Mathematics Education Journal (AMEJ) (Anson, 2021). Australian Council for Computers in Education published the Australian Education Computing journal (Cochrane, 2020) (journal publication is currently paused). Typically, these publications are made available to members in print or online and are only accessible via a subscription. Academics edit the mathematics and computing journals as part of their role in teacher professional associations, and the papers in these journals were blind peer-reviewed before publication. These three papers targeted a specific audience, leaders in independent school settings and in the case of mathematics and computing, the target audience of educators and leaders in schools as well as TEs and teacher education students. The evidence provided supported these educators' decision-making in their day-to-day work deciding on classroom pedagogy, school information and communication policy and developing teacher induction programs.

Three of the publications appear in Teacher Magazine, an online publication produced by the not-for-profit Australian Council for Educational Research (ACER). ACER is funded through commissioned services, including educational research, professional development and assessments (Australian Council for Educational Research (ACER), 2022). Teacher Magazine has a specific wellbeing section of the online journal; two articles were published in this section of the website (Miller,

2021; Smith, 2021). The third article published in Teacher Magazine was submitted as a reader submission (Poeder, 2021), providing space for teachers and educators to share their work. The Teacher magazine website provides a mechanism for teachers to sign up to receive a teacher bulletin to keep up to date with website content. Information on this website is searchable and freely available. The target audience for these papers was practitioners in the field who are working as teachers to provide support for their reflections on their work-life balance and their classroom pedagogy.

Two different commercial publishers published the final three articles. Two were published as a series of articles on teacher job satisfaction in Education Today published by Minnis journal in a section on school management (Greensill, 2020a, 2020b). The third paper in this group was positioned as an opinion piece in the K-12 version of The Educator Australia, an online publication produced by Mumbrella Publishing (Burke, 2021). Most of these publications are freely available and searchable on the publisher's website. The publications targeted leaders and those with the option to influence the development of policy and practice concerning special education curriculum and those with the ability to create space for and support teacher satisfaction.

4.7.2 Embark and Clarify

One of the biggest challenges for the I-STs was identifying and refining a topic of study. The freedom to choose a topic of their interest was a double-edged sword as the I-STs began exploring the literature. The selection of social justice or sustainability in education as a lens to anchor the purpose of the exploration was an essential pedagogical move. Educators as practitioners are problem solvers, and often their immediate response is solution focused. However, in embarking and clarifying a contemporary issue in education we sought to examine and explore a topic and consider what research had to say about it from different angles, perspectives, and worldviews. Hence, the need to move away from our immediate solution focussed response. As an example, an I-ST was concerned about the role of mathematics anxiety and disengagement in her secondary mathematics classroom. The resulting publication identifies the clarified topic she embarked upon as "my learning journey through the literature as I tried to understand mathematics anxiety and related disengagement, and find some suggestions for what I could change in my teaching to support these students so that I could re-engage them with mathematics" (Anson, 2021, p. 12). Miller (2021, p. 2) was concerned about why she and other teachers were "drowning in paperwork" and found "it had never occurred to me how the history of the political influence in education affected us." These examples illustrate the iterative nature of the embarking and clarifying research thinking as evidenced in the published work and provide a context for the ongoing use by the TE to return the I-STs to the three key questions of education being uncertain, purposeful and contributing to human good (Biesta, 2020a).

4.7.3 Find and Generate

Finding out rather than moving towards a solution and sitting with the uncertainty was something most I-ST found novel, as their day-to-day work practices do not allow for time for this longer-term engagement. Sitting with the one issue for an extended period of the semester provided these I-ST with the opportunity to reflect on various voices and viewpoints. The sources of material used in the nine publications identified that finding out what to use was drawn from practice and literature. Several publications used stories of personal or classroom practice. For example, Poeder (2021) shared a classroom moment to illuminate and connect classroom practice with the need for young people to connect with nature. These moments were then also connected to policy and academic literature. In contrast, the academic publications used education theory as a frame to examine a topic and then connect this with practice. For example, Cochrane (2020, p. 2) identified the paper "will investigate the digital divide and domains of capital (Bourdieu, 2002) and discuss how these contribute to impact student access to and use of ICT."

4.7.4 Evaluate and Reflect

Generating ways and means of evaluating levels of trust and weighing up ideas across the range of perspectives from practice and the literature was a challenge for I-STs as they negotiated the different types of publication options. In the context of the newsletter style commercial publications with limited or no options for referencing required careful consideration. Burke's (2021) publication in a commercial newsletter was positioned as an opinion piece focussed on the question "what curriculum is appropriate for students at Special School" (p. 2). To evidence the approach used for evaluating and reflecting on this topic, a problem-solving process was articulated. One of the challenges faced for this publication, where no reference list was included, was providing the structure of the argument and incorporating the evidence used during the reflection. This was typically achieved by referring to key authors by name and institution to explain who has been trusted and why in the text. For example: "… Bruce Knight from Central Queensland University considers the onerous task for teachers and schools to implement and differentiate outcomes" (Burke, 2021, p. 4). This contrasted with the opportunity provided in the journal publications to evidence evaluating the literature in more depth with a focus on identifying both the complexity and limitations of research often evidenced by comparison and contrast. For example, "Research identifies a positive impact on academic achievement for disadvantaged students afforded ubiquitous access to appropriate digital technology at home over a period of time. In contrast, advantaged students who already have access to digital technology at home demonstrate a negligible or even negative impact on academic achievement when provided with additional access to digital technology" (Cochrane, 2020, p. 1).

4.7.5 Organise and Manage

The I-STs began with more short-term notions of engaging with a topic and relied heavily on remembering what they had read recently to generate their responses. Longer term engagement with a topic required a different skill set. Most I-STs were unfamiliar with some of the contemporary electronic tools that can be used to store and manage literature. In our case we used the university supported tool of Endnote to explore how technology could support our management and organisation of what we read and connect it easily to what we write using cite as you write tools. As we progressed throughout the semester our dialogue often shifted to sharing ideas and experiences of what was working and what else might be useful to organise and manage our research thinking. For example, mind mapping of ideas and then generating groups of papers in Endnote on specific topics allowed I-STs to consider the patterns that were emerging in the literature they were reading. This example of pattern identification is evident in the work of Smith (2021) whose literature analysis identified four components of teacher resilience. The four pillars provided the organisational structure for the publication. Similarly, the organisation of a series of publications by Greensill (2020a, 2020b) indicates the ability to group ideas into components to communicate them to the audience of school leaders.

4.7.6 Analyse and Synthesise

Critically synthesising and creating new knowledge was a skill set shift for most first-time postgraduate I-STs. The I-STs needed to consider their own emerging view based on their analysis of what the research says about their topic. For example, in a publication targeted at independent school leaders a summary of the minimum requirements for an induction program were identified as "a mentoring program, structured contextualised reflective practices, school culture training policy and procedure induction" (Andrews, 2021, p. 29). The paper goes on to explain and justify the literature in these three areas and concludes with a call to action for all school leaders "so, the question is, what does you induction program look like" (p. 30).

4.8 Conclusions and Implications

I-STs often find engaging with postgraduate study in their first semester a thought-provoking shift because of their contemporary experience in the field focussed on "what works" and their previous undergraduate experiences of university study. The course offered an opportunity to examine research from different viewpoints and consider what that might mean for different ways of reading, doing, and using research. Being given the freedom to choose in the context of postgraduate study is important for I-STs to connect a topic of importance to them and their practice. Choosing to examine a social justice or sustainability issue meant that I-STs often needed to start to think about their issues in different ways beyond their typical practitioner solution focussed approach. My role as the TE was to challenge examine and question the group and develop their own abilities to engage in these dialogues and engage as a responsive teacher. The group developed the ability to be reflexive and often posed questions and participated in redirection with me as the teacher using Biesta's (2020a) frames of the experimental nature of education, the purposeful nature of education and the possibilities for contributing to human good rather than production.

At the conclusion of the course all I-STs were encouraged to submit their work for publication and to share with group their experiences of the publication process. Some I-STs did not wish to publish their work. However, others submitted and did not hear any response while others are currently undertaking revisions or redefining their work and audience. This ongoing process of publication, review, and reflection outside of the bounds of the formal course of study has attended to my concerns about the temporal nature of education and its impact on I-ST engagement with the cyclical nature of education research. The final assessment task design as a draft, with feedback provided for response, was left incomplete on purpose and provided I-STs the freedom to choose how they engage with their ongoing research thinking. This attested to the notion that the course sought to position professional scholarly writing as a process of production and communication. A further example of I-ST scholarly publication is provided in this book by Brown et al. (Chap. 3). Further research could examine the ways and means to evidence I-ST engagement with the process of communication as process rather than product in the context of postgraduate study.

The course sought to explore a more balanced means of contributing to Biesta's three purposes of education qualifications, socialisation, and subjectification. In this context, participation in the course allowed each person to achieve credit for a required course in their program of study. I also contend that there were opportunities to reflexively engage as an I-ST and researcher to examine research as a social practice in the context of education and engage with the socialisation purpose of education. This aspect also included an examination of both the technical and cultural roles of education research and required responsive teaching pedagogy. The subjectification aspect was something that emerged for some members of the group as they found their voice and engaged with the world in a way that allowed them to be the kind of educator they wanted to be, as illustrated in the work of Miller (2021). These are moments not planned or designed but opportunity that emerge with openness. Hence, I resolve those moments of subjectification can emerge, but I doubt they can be created, and provide an opportunity for further educational research and its role in enabling responsive teaching.

The work of using the RSD framework with postgraduate I-STs required further exploration. Further research can examine the way the development of research skills might operate across a range of disciplines. In my own work, as the first cohort of I-ST reaches the conclusions of the postgraduate study I am keen to engage in some further research that explores the way they have used their newly acquired research skills in their work as a teacher both in terms of their practice and their work with students in the classroom. In addition, some further work is required to examine ways to represent the RSD framework in ways to privilege the cyclical nature of research thinking and overcome the temporal and development challenges identified. The application of the RSD framework provides a means for teachers to be reflective and responsive as they engage with the education as a human event that requires research thinking that explores both the technical and cultural aspects of the practice of teaching.

References

Andrews, T. (2021). Developing a quality induction program for Kairos. *Independence, 46*(2), 28–30. https://independence.partica.online/independence/volume-46-no-2-october-2021/flipbook/30/

Anson, K. (2021). Recognising mathematics anxiety to reduce disengagement in mathematics classrooms. *The Australian Mathematics Education Journal, 3*(2), 12–16.

Australian Council for Educational Research (ACER). (2022). *About ACER*. https://www.acer.org/au/about-us

Australian Education Research Organisation. (2021). *Using evidence*. Australian Education Research Organisation Ltd. Retrieved May 31 from https://www.edresearch.edu.au/using-evidence

Biesta, G. (2015). What is education for? On good education, teacher judgement, and educational professionalism. *European Journal of Education, 50*(1), 75–87. https://doi.org/10.1111/ejed.12109

Biesta, G. (2016). Improving education through research? From effectiveness, causality and technology to purpose, complexity and culture. *Policy Futures in Education, 14*(2), 194–210. https://doi.org/10.1177/1478210315613900

Biesta, G. (2017). *The rediscovery of teaching*. Routledge.

Biesta, G. (2020a). *Educational research: An unorthodox introduction*. Bloomsbury Publishing. https://books.google.com.au/books?id=C56-DwAAQBAJ

Biesta, G. (2020b). Risking ourselves in education: Qualification, socialization, and subjectification revisited. *Educational Theory, 70*(1), 89–104. https://doi.org/10.1111/edth.12411

Biesta, G. (2022). *World-centred education: A view for the present*. Routledge. https://doi.org/10.4324/9781003098331

Bourdieu, P. (2022). The forms of capital. In N. W. Biggart (Ed.), Readings in economic sociology (pp. 280–291). Blackwell Publishers.

Burke, M. (2021). *Opinon: Is there a problem with special school curriculum?* theeducatoronline. Retrieved May 29 from https://www.theeducatoronline.com/k12/news/opinion-is-there-a-problem-with-special-school-curriculum/277386

Cochrane, J. (2020). Factors affecting access to digital technologies and the resulting impact for students in a P-12 context. *Australian Educational Computing, 35*(1). https://journal.acce.edu.au/index.php/AEC/issue/view/14

Gerstl-Pepin, C., & Patrizio, K. (2009). Learning from Dumbledore's pensieve: Metaphor as an aid in teaching reflexivity in qualitative research. *Qualitative Research, 9*(3), 299–308. https://doi.org/10.1177/1468794109105029

Greensill, R. (2020a). *How to build self-efficacy for teacher job satisfaction*. Education Today. Retrieved June 15 from https://www.educationtoday.com.au/news-detail/How-to-build-self-efficacy-for-teacher-job-satisfaction-4962

Greensill, R. (2020b). *Student behaviour and teacher job satisfaction*. Education Today. Retrieved July 15 from https://www.educationtoday.com.au/news-detail/Student-behaviour-and-teacher-job-satisfaction-4994

Griffiths, M. (2012). Why joy in education is an issue for socially just policies. *Journal of Education Policy, 27*(5), 655–670. https://doi.org/10.1080/02680939.2012.710019

Heck, D. (2022). Teacher educators as public intellectuals: Exploring possibilities. *Asia-Pacific Journal of Teacher Education*, 1–12. https://doi.org/10.1080/1359866X.2022.2049700

Krejsler, J. B. (2017). Capturing the 'evidence' and 'what works' agenda in education: A truth regime and the art of manoeuvring floating signifiers. In M. Y. Eryaman, & B. Schneider (Eds.), *Evidence and public good in educational policy, research and practice* (pp. 21–41). Springer International Publishing. https://doi.org/10.1007/978-3-319-58850-6_2

Miles, M. B., Huberman, A. M., & Saldaña, J. (2020). *Qualitative data analysis: A methods sourcebook* (4th ed.). SAGE.

Miller, A. (2021). *The heart and soul of teaching*. Well Being: Teacher. https://www.teachermagazine.com/au_en/articles/the-heart-and-soul-of-teaching

Poeder, M. (2021). *Student engagement with nature—The value of a puddle*. Teacher. Retrieved August 3, 2021, from https://www.teachermagazine.com/au_en/articles/student-engagement-with-nature-the-value-of-a-puddle

Santoro, D. A. (2019). The problem with stories about teacher "burnout." *Kappan, 101*(4), 26–33. https://doi.org/10.1177/0031721719892971

Siegel, S. T., & Biesta, G. (2021). The problem of educational theory. *Policy Futures in Education*, 147821032110320. https://doi.org/10.1177/14782103211032087

Smith, D. (2021). *Four pillars to build your resilience*. Wellbeing by Teacher. Retrieved July 31, from https://www.teachermagazine.com/au_en/articles/four-pillars-to-build-your-resilience

Vanderlinde, R., & van Braak, J. (2010). The gap between educational research and practice: Views of teachers, school leaders, intermediaries and researchers. *British Educational Research Journal, 36*(2), 299–316. https://doi.org/10.1080/01411920902919257

Willison, J., & O'Regan, K. (2007). Commonly known, commonly not known, totally unknown: A framework for students becoming researchers. *Higher Education Research and Development, 26*(4), 393–409.

Willison, J. W. (2018). Research skill development spanning higher education: Critiques, curricula and connections. *Journal of University Teaching and Learning Practice, 15*(4), 1.

Willison, J., & O'Regan, K. (2018). *The Researcher Skill Development Framework*. Retrieved 6/622 from https://www.adelaide.edu.au/melt/ua/media/771/rsd7_15april2018.pdf

Woore, R., Mutton, T., & Molway, L. (2020). 'It's definitely part of who I am in the role'. Developing teachers' research engagement through a subject-specific Master's programme. *Teacher Development, 24*(1), 88–107. https://doi.org/10.1080/13664530.2019.1693421

Deborah Heck is as an Associate Professor in the School of Education and Tertiary Access. She is passionate about working with teachers, including those who are seeking entry to the profession and those exploring how to take the next step and develop their own research. Deborah researches problems that are emerging in teacher education, teaching and higher education practice.

Open Access This chapter is licensed under the terms of the Creative Commons Attribution 4.0 International License (http://creativecommons.org/licenses/by/4.0/), which permits use, sharing, adaptation, distribution and reproduction in any medium or format, as long as you give appropriate credit to the original author(s) and the source, provide a link to the Creative Commons license and indicate if changes were made.

The images or other third party material in this chapter are included in the chapter's Creative Commons license, unless indicated otherwise in a credit line to the material. If material is not included in the chapter's Creative Commons license and your intended use is not permitted by statutory regulation or exceeds the permitted use, you will need to obtain permission directly from the copyright holder.

Chapter 5
Research-Oriented University Instruction: The Research Skill Development Framework and Communities of Practice

Sylvia Tiala and Kara Loy

Abstract To address higher education teaching efficacy, this chapter describes how the Research Skill Development (RSD) framework has been successfully applied to underpin professional development programs, namely through Communities of Practice (CoP) that explore research-thinking and a host of research-oriented teaching practices in two universities. These universities are, respectively, located on the Canadian prairie and in the Midwestern United States. In our professional roles, we provide professional development for university educators (UEs) across all disciplines and modalities. The RSD framework sparked interest amongst university educator participants by encouraging discourse on research thinking and by providing a common language to interrogate existing practice and to envision new teaching possibilities. The RSD framework catalysed and supported individual and group research thinking. In turn, university educators engaged with research-oriented teaching practices and publishing on teaching practice in the field of Scholarship of Teaching and Learning (SoTL). Our findings indicated that lasting and meaningful change to research-thinking, in research-oriented teaching practices, and in SoTL, can be enabled through CoP that are underpinned and guided by the RSD framework. This chapter positions the RSD as a valuable and strategic tool for improving teaching while mitigating changing university agendas and concomitant challenges.

Keyword University educators · Teaching and learning centres · Professional development · Communities of practice · Scholarship of teaching and learning (SoTL) · Research skill development (RSD)

S. Tiala (✉)
University of Wisconsin–Stout, Menomonie, USA
e-mail: tialas@uwstout.edu

K. Loy (✉)
Coast Mountain College, Terrace, Canada
e-mail: kloy@coastmountaincollege.ca

5.1 Background

Higher education and academic sectors comprise two principal audiences, university students and those who teach them. University educators (UEs) come from a range of disciplines. Included in the student audience, within Faculties or Schools of Education, are preservice teachers (in undergraduate and master's programs) who intend to join the workforce as Pre-K to grade 12 teachers. There are also students enrolled in master's programs who are already school teachers (In-service teachers or ISTs). All those who teach in university degree-granting programs, including in schools and faculties of education programs, are called here UEs and they are the focus of this chapter.

Many UEs are not substantially trained in pedagogical practices, with their training focusing on research. These UEs may have limited teaching experience or limited exposure to instructional theories and practices. To overcome such gaps in experience and exposure, most universities, including the two discussed in this chapter, maintain university teaching and learning centres (TLCs) aimed at creating institutional environments that are responsive to improving UE's teaching and students' learning.

The professional development (PD) activities described in this chapter focus on forming and sustaining Communities of Practice (CoP) wherein UEs come together as a cohort with a facilitator or guide to explore and evolve their teaching practice over a period of time (Lave & Wenger, 1991; Taylor et al., 2021). Facilitation of the CoPs described here utilized six facets of the Research Skill Development (RSD) framework (Willison & O'Regan, 2006, 2018). The RSD framework provided an adaptable, flexible pedagogical tool that was well suited to catalyse and support responsive teaching utilizing research-oriented pedagogies. Research-oriented pedagogies have been a growing area of interest across universities in North America and internationally (Kenny, 1998; Jenkins & Healey, 2018). RSD-informed CoPs engaged participants in cooperative and interactive PD through exposure to research-oriented instructional techniques and tenets. The authors found that the RSD framework proved an effective mechanism to develop responsive teaching practices by sparking and sustaining participants' interest and helping TLCs identify and consolidate good teaching/learning practices. The RSD framework provided a common language for UEs to communicate across disciplines, interrogate and reflect on existing practice, and respond quickly to immediate needs of instructors and institutional environments.

5.1.1 University Educators and Research Thinking

TLCs PD activities usually involve workshops, training sessions or event series, expert speakers, micro-credentials, one-to-one consultations and CoP. Typically, activities help educators find and clarify evidence-based theories and teaching practices.

5 Research-Oriented University Instruction: The Research Skill ...

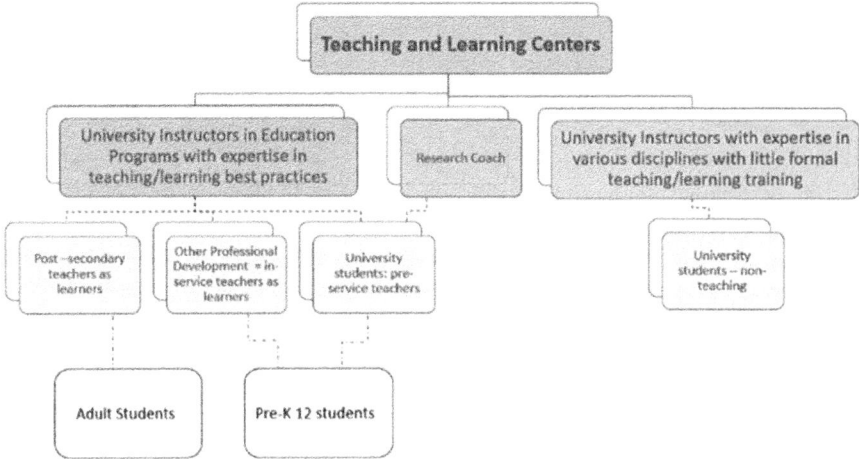

Fig. 5.1 University educator's professional development ties to preservice and in-service teachers involved in pre-K to 12 education systems

Figure 5.1 illustrates how TLCs target UEs as the primary audience for PD activities while being cognizant that the reason is to impact students' learning through improved and responsive teaching. The primary audience is complemented by graduate students with teaching responsibilities or undergraduate students where they are specifically enlisted as teaching assistants or research coaches. UEs' students then form the secondary audience and include pre-and in-service teachers with the potential to impact students in pre-K to twelfth grade schooling. Teachers may also impact, adult learners in other contexts, such as polytechnics or business training.

We apply *research thinking and responsive teaching* as conceptual tools in the educational development of UEs. They inform "teaching as a habit of respond[ing] dynamically to students' diverse needs and the evolving demands on their lives" (Willison, Chap. 1 of this book), including the habit of foresight and responsiveness in course-design and in implementation and assessment of student learning. Research thinking, as described by the six facets of the RSD framework, positions educators to "react... to contingencies and systematically adapt their practice through consolidation and change" over time (Willison, Chap. 1 of this book). Related to research thinking is research-oriented teaching, denoting a set of strategies that elicit student research skill development. Two vignettes, shared here, describe how research-oriented teaching skills are developed with UEs at two different universities.

5.2 Vignettes

Our first vignette comes from an Institute for Teaching and Learning (ITL) at a research-intensive university in Canada supporting the learning of over 30,000 students. Academic staff at the ITL is responsible for advancing responsive teaching and learning emphasizing development of instructional capacity around experiential learning (EL). Undergraduate research is a key component of EL and involves course-based research experiences along with faculty-mentored studentships and assistantships. ITL academic staff seeks to build instructional capacity across high impact practices (Kuh, 2008) by providing workshops, online learning modules, practical guides, and CoP. One aim was to respond to institutional goals for integrating experiential learning specifically increasing curricular opportunities for undergraduate research through an initiative called Course-based Undergraduate Research Experience, or CURE.

Our second vignette is from an American Midwestern polytechnic university's Teaching and Learning Center (MTLC) supporting the learning of more than 7500 students. This vignette focuses on how the MTLC staff helped educators integrate evidence-based and high-impact (Kuh, 2008) practices into their teaching in response to the university's mission to provide learners with discipline-specific skills and professional competencies.

Both the MTLC and the ITL employed Willison and O'Regan's (2006, 2018) RSD-framework with communities-of-practice (Lave & Wenger, 1991). The activities and deliverables across the two contexts were conceived of and executed independently of one another. Surveys and interviews in both contexts were used to gauge impact on UEs' responsive approaches to teaching and on students' research thinking and research skill development.

5.2.1 Vignette 1: Finding a CURE

ITL was tasked in 2020 with expanding opportunities for students to engage in course-based undergraduate research experience (CURE), comprising research, scholarship, artistic exploration, inquiry-based learning, design and prototyping. The guidelines for quality curricular undergraduate research at the institution were informed by definitions put forward by the Council on Undergraduate Research (CUR, 2021).

One mechanism for expanding opportunities was to invite UEs to participate in PD aimed to enable them to design and implement CURE in an existing course. The ITL reported that over a two-year period, 12 educators became involved in the PD and CoP. Eleven of these 12 university educators went on to offer CURE in courses they taught. Across four semesters they reached more than 1700 undergraduate students. Program evaluation captured the impact on the UEs' participants including changes to their practice, connections across peers and colleagues, and impacts on student learning.

UEs in the CoP were provided content and resources that empowered them with a curated set of foundational resources, strategies, examples, and PD exercises. Educators were exposed to the RSD frameworks (Willison & O'Regan, 2006, 2018) in terms of how these could be used in teaching practices where undergraduate research was a pedagogical strategy. Educators explored assumptions, values and responsiveness around teaching, research, student skills, and students' prior knowledge. They embarked and clarified research-focused learning outcomes, found and generated learning activities, and organised logistics and assessment protocols. Educators were provided with examples to critique and to inform their own designs for either online or in-person teaching contexts.

The RSD-enriched PD stressed the importance of cultivating a community of student researchers, inclusion of student collaboration, and communication of research findings on the part of students. UEs discussed critical reflection and authentic assessment as means for consolidating students' research-oriented learning. Throughout, UEs were invited to consider and discuss topics such as subjectivity in assessment, different epistemologies, and the effects of student well-being on learning.

5.2.2 Vignette 2: Caching the RSD

A group of UEs across MTLC's campus actively engaged from 2014 to 2021 in promoting undergraduate research as a best and high impact practice (Kuh, 2008). Efforts to enhance student learning resulted in a student senate resolution to incorporate undergraduate research as a signature experience; participating at a system-level in a National Science Foundation-funded series promoting undergraduate research; and a Chancellor's directive to provide PD for UEs focusing on undergraduate research. In response to these initiatives, the MTLC's PD focused on building expertise for UEs beginning with a common definition of research and on developing research experiences for students. John Willison (of Willison & O'Regan, 2006) visited MTLC's campus, conducted a multi-day workshop helping UEs understand, and explicitly communicate, six facets of research skills to their learners. After Willison's visit, a multi-disciplinary team of UEs and educational librarians spent an academic year in a community of practice (CoP) creating responsive teaching environments using the RSD framework in their own contexts. Participants sought out and adapted resources for their own use and employed scholarship of teaching and learning (SoTL) strategies to evaluate the effectiveness of employing the RSD framework in their instructional practices.

Eighteen months after Willison's visit, UEs and an academic librarian from the MTLC-sponsored RSD CoP, helped other UEs integrate undergraduate research experiences into their own instruction using geocaching as a simile for integrating research skills into instruction. The aim of the exercise was to engage participants in the research process, problem solve as a team, communicate effectively, and participate in active learning processes that mirrored elements of the RSD framework. The caching activity culminated in UEs being asked to connect the RSD framework to the activity they had just experienced, reflect on the types of communication that occurred, and share how the RSD framework and the workshop experience might enhance student learning in their individual contexts.

5.2.3 Approach for RSD

In both vignettes, there was an impetus for institutional change. Key staff, including teaching and learning centre directors and academic staff working as academic developers or administrators, examined the institutional environment, considered the social infrastructure and cultures, and consciously chose the RSD framework as a foundational framework to respond to the demands of the institution while addressing the needs of instructors and students. The rest of this chapter focuses on the efficacy of PD programming across the two universities. We identify how two teaching and learning centres integrated the RSD framework into their PD and articulate the effectiveness of creating responsive teaching environments.

Experience with the RSD framework indicates that individuals need time to engage with, implement, and refine RSD-related practices in order to become confident and competent. The U-TLC in this chapter gauged their impact by collecting qualitative and quantitative feedback and surveying past participants in RSD-related PD. The results provide a glimpse of PD impacts across institutions and provide insights for other teaching and learning centres interested in responding to their own institutional environments.

The efficacy of CoP is achieved through features termed "collegial, flexible, reciprocal and generous" (Taylor et al., 2021, para 17). The qualities and internal influence of CoP as PD tools for research-oriented teaching and thinking, and based on the RSD framework, respond to additional factors affecting institutional environments including leadership, strategic plans, disciplinary epistemologies, and institutional cultures.

5.3 Methodology

Both qualitative and quantitative data were used to examine the effects that RSD-related CoP and other RSD-related PD initiatives have on UEs perceptions of effectiveness and student learning in the ITL and MTLC contexts. Weaving qualitative and quantitative data together across contexts allows teaching and learning centres to consider impacts through a broader, institutional environment (Taylor et al., 2021). As Willison asserted, "to enact effective change, consideration must be given to the ecology of learning, where changing one aspect of learning may have an impact on other key aspects" (Chap. 2, p. 31). While it has been established that student learning is affected vis-à-vis extended engagement in capacity building for academic educators and UEs through communities-of-practice, collating evidence relative to the student experience or institutional value happens through noting changes to language, value, and practices (Roxå et al., 2011).

5.4 Results and Discussion

We tie our analysis of PD and its impact on UEs and students using elements of a framework for integrated teaching & learning networks (Taylor et al., 2021; Roxå & Mårtensson, 2013; Pyörälä et al., 2015; Pataraia et al., 2015; Willison, 2012). As well, we tend to the themes of consolidation, change and connections (Willison, see Chap. 1) in the context of systemically supporting responsive institutional environments.

Qualitative data was collected at ITL by way of formal and informal debriefing sessions with individual and small groups of UEs. Data was provided by UEs who had participated in PD that emphasized the RSD framework and who had gone on to implement CURE. Respondents were invited to comment on the efficacy of the PD and provide insights on the value of the RSD framework and aspects of the support provided in relation to perceived effects on student learning. Over 30 responses came from debriefing sessions, with some UEs participating multiple times. Quantitative and qualitative data on effects on student learning is briefly summarized.

The MTLC collected quantitative data using a survey sent to 89 educators who participated in RSD-related PD between the years of 2014 and 2021. The PD included hour-long workshops, multiple-day symposia, and a year-long CoP. Twenty-five respondents identified the number and type of RSD-related sessions they participated in, the level of engagement they felt during these sessions, the number of students impacted as a result of their participating, and their comfort levels using the RSD framework in research—related class activities (teaching, assessment, and integration). UEs were also asked to identify impacts of RSD PD programming on their teaching and students' learning.

Twenty-five UEs responses were categorized according to the self-reported number of students impacted. Twelve UEs (48%) provided answers such as "very few", indicating an amount fewer than 10, or leaving the question blank. These UEs and their subsequent answers to other questions were assigned to a group we refer to as "Low", as in a low number-of-students-were-impacted. Seven UEs indicated that their work with the RSD framework had impacted 10 to 99 students and were assigned to the "Medium" impact group. Six UEs indicated that their RSD-related efforts impacted 100 or more students with as many as 2000 students impacted. This group of UEs and their subsequent responses were assigned to the "High" impact group. We recognize that respondents may have engaged with the RSD framework over a longer time span than others who were introduced to the RSD framework more recently. Some UEs indicated that Covid-19 impacted their ability to engage in research activities. The number of students reported as impacted may not accurately reflect UEs level of interest or intended commitment to enhance student learning using the RSD framework.

5.4.1 University Educators' Consolidation

In CoP, social interactions, self-reflection, and peer processing help build microcultures (Taylor et al., 2021) that support educators' consolidation of new information and actionable results in the classroom. One-off presentations or workshops are used to pique interest and draw UEs into a longer-term commitment to PD and practice. An assumption made by TLCs is that if educators are more engaged in PD, they are more likely to create responsive teaching environments that positively impact their students.

In the MTLC context, university educators' patterns for engaging in RSD-related activities from 2014 to 2021 were analysed according to number of students impacted ("Low" = 0 – 9; "Medium" = 10 – 99; "High" = 100 +). Participation rates for educators in "Low", "Medium", and "High" student impact groups was an average of the number of PD opportunities attended (presentations, workshops, symposia, CoP).

Educators in the "Low" group (n = 12) averaged 1.7 PD opportunities over the course of seven years. Educators in the "Medium" group (n = 7) averaged 4.9 PD opportunities, while respondents in the "High" group (n = 6) averaged 3.8 PD activities over the course of seven years (see Fig. 5.2). Participation in sharing communities and CoP represented year-long commitments so participation averages (amount of opportunities/number of participants) was reported as 1.57 and 1.50 for the "Medium" and "High" groups indicating multiple commitments exploring the RSD framework were sustained over time.

Survey comments from participants more engaged with RSD-related PD reported that the RSD framework was easy for both educators and students to understand. They appreciated the RSD-enriched PD opportunities as a way to build community and collaborate with others.

Evidence that CoP help build a positive learning environment and a microculture of responsive teaching (Taylor et al., 2021) is reflected in MTLC UEs' self-reported comfort level ratings (0 = not at all/5 = extremely comfortable) in teaching the RSD framework, assessing students using the RSD framework, and integrating the RSD into student research (see Fig. 5.3).

UEs in the "Medium" and "High" groups were more comfortable teaching with the RSD framework than educators in the "Low" group. Assessed comfort levels using the RSD framework and integrating RSD-related instruction into student research for the "Medium" and "High" impact groups was more than twice the level of their "Low" impact counterparts. This stands to reason as more engagement in RSD-related PD is intentionally designed to increase confidence using new teaching methodologies. Participants from the "Low" student impact group reflected minimal engagement with the RSD. Some UEs did not use, or remember using, the RSD framework with

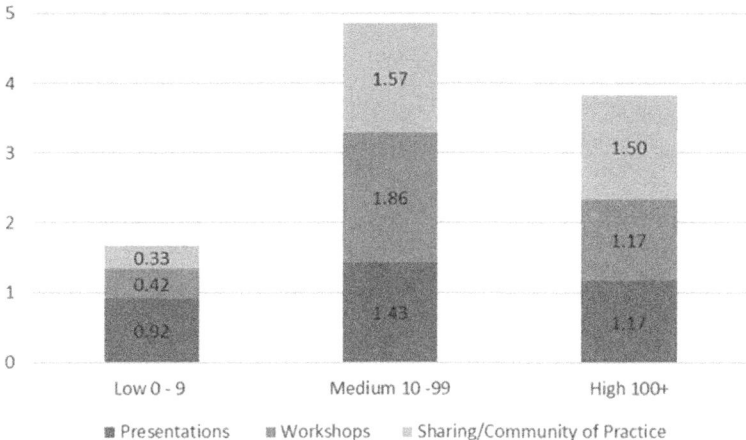

Fig. 5.2 Average UE RSD—related professional development participation by student impact

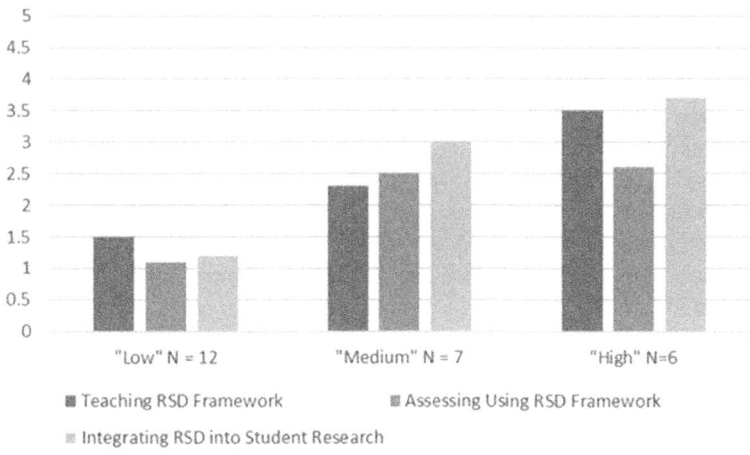

Fig. 5.3 University educators' comfort levels teaching, assessing and integrating the RSD framework

students. One UEs used the framework to locate program redundancies and observe the value of strategies being implemented. The other UEs in the "Low" impact group found the framework difficult to understand, not applicable to their situation; and a majority (9/12) remained silent on the uses or benefits of using the RSD framework.

In contrast, all participants in the "Medium" and "High" impact groups were able to reflect on ways programming impacted their teaching. Responses affirmed increased attention to clarifying expectations, matching course expectations with assessments, scaffolding assignments across courses and programs, and incorporating information literacy into research assignments. Reflecting on, and changing, practices was a repeating theme. UEs reported moving away from traditional research papers toward "more visual representation of … data" or indicated that the experience "gave me more user-friendly methods of teaching research, which was valued by my students". Most notably, one UE tied the RSD-related PD to the university's polytechnic mission stating that, "applied research is fundamental to my students' careers and this framework helped me make it more career-based, field-grounded, and practical".

In the ITL context, qualitative indicators revealed that consolidation of meaning was sometimes immediate and substantive for UEs as a result of RSD-enriched PD and CoP. At other times, effects were incremental or delayed. Sometimes, consolidation and meaning making occurred as a mechanism of guided group debriefs, a component of the ITL program evaluation of CURE. Several respondents mentioned limits to consolidation around research and teaching with one educator noting that, "…taking some elements from CURE and integrat[ing] it with… the other way we teach, I haven't thought about this because it takes time even to conceptualize CURE, it has so many components, so many things to do, you have just three months. But, maybe intuitively, it is possible right?". Another UE mentioned the challenge of consolidating the RSD-PD this way, "We're always encouraged to do new things, try new stuff, integrate new processes, [but] we spend very little time reflecting on if it works".

A UE who participated in more than one CoP, and who implemented CURE in multiple courses, reflected on how she consolidated research and teaching into her professional praxis and identity, "I would say,…, offering CUREs has been an important part of my life teaching and research practice for the past six years, so it definitely helps form…my teaching identity and my professional identity".

Another UE spoke about how participating in the RSD-enriched PD and CoP resulted in an ability to consolidate substantial pedagogical innovation in a shorter period of time, "… it helped accelerate that process so something that may have taken me another couple of years, I was able to accomplish relatively quickly, and now I can just build upon it and continue that process in years to come". Yet, he still wished for more time, "Even though I thought about it for a while and this was kind of meshed with ideas that I previously had, time was tight, and it would have been much, much better if I'd had more time to think about it, like if I had a half a year led in to develop this".

Overall, UEs participating in the RSD-enriched PD and CoP felt impeded by time around implementing CURE, as well as pressures pertaining to the COVID-19 pandemic. Still, consolidation of PD is best supported through sustained educational development, including CoP, that can become more evident over time.

5.4.2 University Educators' Change

Within two years of enhanced efforts on RSD-relevant PD, a substantial change in teaching practice was found to have shifted institutional microcultures. Twelve UEs took part in two consecutive CoP and went on to offer more than 1700 undergraduate students a course-based research experience (CURE) across four academic semesters between 2020 and 2022.

Five of six UEs in one debriefing and evaluation cycle agreed that their research thinking was impacted as a result of the PD and CoP. Specifically, UEs were asked "what was your understanding at the beginning about the goals of the CURE [PD] and did your understanding change by the end of the course [three sessions]?". Respondents indicated that their thinking changed and opened up around emergent effects for learners and for effects regarding teaching large classes. For instance, one UE noted, "I was really open to changes into any shape that will emerge, and I think [the CURE] was quite useful in the sense that I could incorporate it from there; I don't imagine that class without [a CURE] you know, because it was so fundamental to imagine". Another UE summarized their changes in thinking and practice referencing the RSD framework facets in this way:

> That workshop really helped me to understand the goals of CURE and also it deepened my understanding...our focus goes to the data analysis, this and that, but through the seminar what I realized [is] that, 'okay, there is a first step so it is the question itself, and the question should come from the student's mind', ...and this was the most difficult part actually.

Similarly, another UE specified that, "my understanding radically changed from the first time I ran a CURE to the second time...and also a bit about just the feasibility of being able to run CURES in larger courses and yeah, I spend more time thinking about those things". This same UE referred to a deepening understanding of his role in supporting undergraduates as researchers across the RSD facets noting that, "When you do research... our students have a certain level, so ...in the [RSD-inclusive work] book she sent us; so there are different levels. *How [do] you grow as a researcher?* It is level one, level two. So, that was very helpful for me". Further, this UE noted, "So this is a different type of pedagogy that now I'm learning; I'm implementing learning from the mistakes and so on, so this will surely help me grow as a teacher [,] as an instructor".

In contrast to the experiences captured here, some UEs and staff participated in the ITL PD and CoP but did not subsequently offer a CURE. Included in this group are staff working in the co-curricular space such as with the campus sustainability unit, and UEs who did not go on to be assigned a course that fit with offering CURE. These individuals did not participate in the debrief and evaluation, so their experiences are beyond the scope of this chapter.

In contrast to the qualitative data ITL collected, MTLC used a quantitative approach to assess evidence in growth of thinking or change in practice as reported by UE. Evidence for responsive teaching was drawn from the number of courses UEs altered, posters presented, presentations made, articles published, or workshops led as the result of the RSD PD or CoP. A total of 73 actions (Fig. 5.4) were a result of RSD-related PD. Thirty-five courses were altered, eight posters were presented, 18 conference presentations were delivered, two publications were accepted, and 10 workshops were offered.

In altering courses, we looked across groups of UEs with impacts on "Low", "Medium", or "High" numbers of students depending on how many courses were

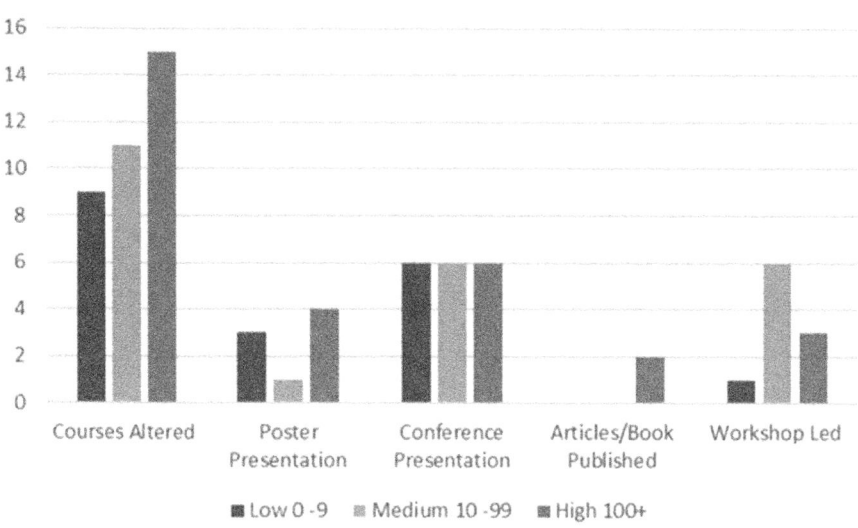

Fig. 5.4 Evidence of university educator growth by professional development category

altered. Twelve educators who indicated they only impacted a "Low" number of students collectively altered 9 courses (0.75/each). Seven educators who impacted a "Medium" number of students collectively altered 11 courses (1.57/each). Meanwhile educators impacting a "High" number of students collectively altered 15 courses (2.5/each). It is clear that there is a relationship between the number of courses altered and the number of students impacted. Interestingly, there are three poster presentations and six conference presentations evident for UE respondents who indicated a low number of students involved. On closer analysis, evidence of professional impact also came from UEs who indicated a high level of engagement (3.4–5) with RSD-related PD without indicating how many students were impacted by their instruction. It is possible that these respondents were actively engaging with the RSD framework but impacted few students and/or are incorrectly categorized into the "Low" impact group.

Impacts to knowledge flow and the institutional environment (Taylor et al., 2021) were found in MTLC survey responses that reflected institutional longer-term vision and strategy. One UE participant spoke to strategizing ways to leverage their PD experience by stating, *"I learned and valued this hands-on, professional, and positive experience. I have indirectly, yet holistically incorporated the professional development experience into my teaching, research, and service. Further, I have indirectly, yet holistically incorporated [the RSD framework] into my administration and accreditation work too"*. A second UE participant spoke to strengthening existing work and visioning future PD opportunities indicating that,

> Having the RSD framework to encourage student activity in research has strengthen[ed] this course component. I would like to learn more and engage with other instructors/professors [university educators] who are using it. I like the flexibility of the framework and while I

might not use all of the components, I will continue to learn how to implement it better when workshops and other supports continue.

5.4.3 University Educators' Connections

Communities of practice (CoP) create microcultures and connections (Taylor et al., 2021) critical to successfully implementing responsive change in the learning ecosystem at a university. UEs are willing to work with others across disciplines but frequently need a structured experience to facilitate constructive and collaborative conversations. Creating generative spaces where UEs can meet others, develop relationships, experiment with strategies, and commit to consistent meeting times are functions that teaching and learning centres easily facilitate. CoP, such as those related to the RSD framework in the contexts described here, created group hubs and microcultures influencing institutional environments that persist across UE attrition, changes in administration, and shifting institutional priorities. Analysis of MTLC and ITL revealed that university teaching and learning centers were both able to impact institutional teaching and learning ecosystems, and the associated knowledge flow, by creating connections across disciplines, with new and existing resources, including among a growing number of experts in CURE.

One UE who reflected deeply on the professional and student benefits of participating in the RSD-enriched PD also shared the experience of coordinating CURE in a large, multi-section engineering course. He noted further sharing his knowledge throughout his department at an event that highlighted teaching innovations, and through mentorship to contract UE. In so doing, he faced both collegial resistance and support from the department head for "trying new things".

In terms of benefits, other UE participants in the ITL RSD-enriched PD noted multiple advantages relating to connections to peers equally or potentially invested in research thinking and teaching practices related to undergraduate research. One UE offering CURE in a senior seminar in communications found like-minded colleagues through the PD, "I am absolutely passionate about undergraduate research, so the direct benefit I felt [was] that there are other people as committed". This educator continued to emphasize how this kind of PD empowered UE, including her, to promote research-oriented pedagogy within department networks and that more was needed:

> I was the only one; nobody really understood what it [CURE] is. But one of the things that I would suggest is more promotion of this because some people could really benefit, and they had no clue… so I try to promote it. We need to promote undergraduate research, so I became quite a proponent…I'm a fan of the [CURE CoP] program.

5.4.4 Impacts on Student Learning

Students enrolled in courses involving CURE from 2020 to 2022 were invited to respond to online surveys. Of approximately 1780 enrolled students, 92 participated in the optional surveys. Survey questions were informed by the skill facets of the RSD (Willison & O'Regan, 2006, 2018) specifically asking students about their abilities to analyse and synthesize as well as communicate and apply. Ninety-one of the 92 respondents agreed or strongly agreed that they were able to analyse/interpret data as a result of their course-based research experience. All 92 respondents indicated that they had communicated their research experience within their social networks. Respondents also indicated that the research experiences offered them a valuable learning experience (mean of 6.4 on a Likert scale of 7) and that the research experience helped them develop their academic skills (mean of 6.2). Over 70% of the respondents indicated that the research experience helped them to communicate research-based information and develop an ability to collaborate, build relationships and work with others. The survey concluded with three open-ended questions inviting respondents to complete the prompt: *As a result of this research experience, I …; This research experience helped to develop …; and Participating in a research experience meant …*. Students' submissions provided insight into their thinking across the skill facets of Willison & O'Regan's (2006, 2018) RSD Frameworks.

We return to MTCL to illustrate UEs' perceptions of student learning. Most survey respondents (12 of 13) from the "Medium" and "High" groups identified tangible impacts on student learning. One theme evident from the responses was students' improved understanding of research and utilization of research processes both inside and outside of the classroom. As one UE respondent indicated, "Students saw the value of how research can be used in their careers and in various field settings. They learned best practices that they can easily recall and apply in their future courses and careers". Students were more successful in submitting quality papers or projects with better writing as clearer expectations around assignments were provided. Several UEs mentioned an improvement in information literacy skills indicating a concerted effort to connect research skills with information literacy. Increased metacognition relating to the research process, including critical thinking, more interesting projects, and more project depth, were identified as impacts on student learning. This increase in critical thinking may be connected to UEs restructuring courses to provide more autonomy for students around choice of research topics and dissemination activities such as presentations to the local community, classmates, and invited guests during university-sponsored research day. As one respondent indicated, "I believe that the students have a deeper understanding of the… topic that they research[ed] using RSD. They become stronger critical thinkers [and]… told me that they really enjoy delving into a topic of their choice".

Even though evidence comes from two separately facilitated CoP at two separate institutions, we note that commensurability across impact signals the RSD framework as a valuable tool in PD or educational development of UEs' responsive teaching environments.

5.5 Conclusion

Both challenges and opportunities remain in creating institutionally responsive PD. Specifically, we have identified three challenges. Firstly, it is fraught to thoroughly evidence direct and indirect impact on student learning because the UEs as participant in PD is the main audience and students are the secondary audience. Secondly, despite the benefits of extended engagement with UEs through CoP, it can be challenging to sustain or resource these communities as priorities, needs, and energies shift within and across units and institutions. Finally, it can be challenging to sustain CoP because of top-down or outside-in changes to priorities and trends. There can be undue focus on a new tool or strategy, or there can be a deemphasizing of previous priorities related to changes in leadership. New trends can too easily supplant tried and true resources, including the RSD framework.

Investing in extended capacity building through communities-of-practice requires finding, generating, synthesizing, and communicating evidence of its efficacy and value not only for individual UEs but broadly for the benefit of the student experience, and for institutions holistically (Raffoul et al., 2022). Shifting expectations, modalities, priorities, and increasing workloads affect UEs, often negatively. Yet, as institutional priorities evolve, the RSD framework remains viable across trends and changing priorities.

Changing priorities impacted both contexts illustrated here and included changes to institutional leadership, changes in political climates, and shifting pedagogical foci during the time frames referenced. Institutional memory was threatened or even lost during multiple years of budget reductions, austerity measures, and the retirement or resignations of UEs and administrators committed to undergraduate research. The one constant element during times of fluctuating priorities was the MTLC & ITC academic staff who helped consolidate and sustain efforts as RSD-competent UEs left or changed their priorities.

Professional and academic development is a journey, not an end in itself. We recommend centres and educational developers consider launching and sustaining communities of practice that cultivate relationships for teachers, pre-service teachers, and UEs. We also recommend UEs continue engagement with scholarship of teaching and learning (SoTL) to remain responsive and continually interrogate what is, or can be, efficacious in terms of RSD-framework informed practice in teaching, learning and research. We note the value of providing for institutional cultures through the development of and support for integrated networks of educators and students (Taylor et al., 2021) as mechanisms to sustain learning ecologies across institutions. Regarding theoretical implications, we recommend further research into the nuances and diversities across professional micro-cultures and communities of practice. In turn, these investigations can be generative SoTL contributions. The PD activities and relationships that spark and sustain research thinking and research-oriented teaching practices evolve in concert, and these are of utmost importance to pursue in universities, especially in times of rapid and wide-reaching change.

References

Committee on Defining Deeper Learning and 21st Century Skills. (2012). *Education for life and work: Developing transferable knowledge and skills in the 21st century*. National Academies Press.

Council on Undergraduate Research (2021). Council on Undergraduate Research Issues Updated Definition of Undergraduate Research. https://www.cur.org/council-on-undergraduate-research-issues-updated-definition-of-undergraduate-research/

Darling-Hammond, L., Hyler, M. E., & Gardner, M. (2017). *Effective teacher professional development*. https://learningpolicyinstitute.org/sites/default/files/product-files/Effective_Teacher_Professional_Development_REPORT.pdf

Flanagan, K., Braun, R., Cantin, A., Loy, K., & Summers, M. (2022). *A guide for undergraduate research at UCalgary*. University of Calgary, Taylor Institute for Teaching and Learning Guide Series. https://taylorinstitute.ucalgary.ca/resources/a-guide-for-undergraduate-research-at-ucalgary

Jenkins, A., & Healey, M. (2018). The role of academic developers in embedding high-impact undergraduate research and inquiry in mainstream higher education: Twenty years' reflection. *International Journal for Academic Development, 23*(1), 52–64. https://doi.org/10.1080/1360144X.2017.1412974

Kaipainen, E., Braun, R., & Arseneault, R. (2020). *University of Calgary, Taylor Institute of Teaching and Learning, Experiential Learning Plan*. https://ucalgary.ca/provost/sites/default/files/EL%20Plan%202020-25.pdf

Kenny, S. S., (1998). The Boyer commission on educating undergraduates in the research university: Reinventing undergraduate education: A blueprint for America's research universities. https://files.eric.ed.gov/fulltext/ED424840.pdf

Kuh, G. D. (2008). *High-impact educational practices: What they are, who has access to them, and why they matter*. Association of American Colleges and Universities.

Lave, J., & Wenger, E. (1991). *Situated learning: Legitimate peripheral participation*. Cambridge University Press.

Loy, K. (2022). Undergraduate research in Canada. In J. Lehmann, & H. Mieg (Eds.), *Cambridge handbook of undergraduate research*. Cambridge University Press.

Loy, K., Tiala, S., & Massie, M., (2021, November 27–Dec 2). Strategies and solutions using the research skill development framework to promote campus-wide research-oriented teaching and cultural shifts. Australian Association for Research in Education (AARE), Reimagining Education Research: Brisbane, Australia (virtual). Conference presentation.

Mckenna, A. F., Johnson, A. M., Yoder, B., Chavela Guerra, R. C., & Pimmel, R. (2016, January). Evaluating virtual communities of practice for faculty development. *The Journal of Faculty Development, 30*(1), 31–40.

Moore, J. L., & Felten, P. (2018). Academic development in support of mentored undergraduate research and inquiry. *The International Journal for Academic Development, 23*, 1.

Pataraia, N., Margaryan, A., Falconer, I., & Littlejohn, A. (2015). How and what do academics learn through their personal networks. *Journal of Further and Higher Education, 39*(3), 336–357. https://doi.org/10.1080/0309877X.2013.831041

Pyörälä, E., Hirsto, L., Toom, A., Myyry, L., & Lindblom-Ylänne, S. (2015). Significant networks and meaningful conversations observed in the first-round applicants for the Teachers' Academy at a research-intensive university. *International Journal for Academic Development, 20*(2), 150–162. https://doi.org/10.1080/1360144X.2015.1029484

Raffoul, J., Loy, K., Hoessler, C., Kolomitro, K., Ives, C., & Groen, J. (2022). Use of narratives to communicate value in educational development. *Journal on Centers for Teaching and Learning, 14*, 90–105.

Roxå, T., & Mårtensson, K. (2013). Understanding strong academic microcultures: An exploratory study. CED, Centre for Educational Development, Lunds University. https://lucris.lub.lu.se/ws/files/55148513/Microcultures_eversion.pdf

Roxå, T., Mårtenssen, K., & Alveteg, M., (2011). Understanding and influencing teaching and learning cultures at university: A network approach. *Higher Education, 62*, 99–111.

Schön, D. A. (1983). *The reflective practitioner: How professionals think in action*. Basic Books.

Taylor, K. L., Kenny, N. A., Perrault, E., & Mueller, R. A. (2021). Building integrated networks to develop teaching and learning: the critical role of hubs. *International Journal for Academic Development*. https://doi.org/10.2080/1360144X.2021.189931

Willison, J. (2012). When academics integrate research skill development in the curriculum. *Higher Education Research & Development, 31*(6), 905–919. https://doi.org/10.1080/07294360.2012.658760

Willison, J. (2020). *The models of engaged learning and teaching*. Springer.

Willison, J., & O'Regan, K. (2006, 2018). *Researcher skill development framework*. https://www.adelaide.edu.au/melt/ua/media/765/rsd_4nov19.pdf

Wuetherick, B. (2020). Transforming undergraduate research at Canadian universities. In N. H. Hensel, & P. Blessinger (Eds.), *International perspectives on undergraduate research* (pp. 265–280). Palgrave Macmillan. https://doi.org/10.1007/978-3-030-53559-9_15

Sylvia Tiala is the Director of the Nakatani Teaching and Learning Center at the University of Wisconsin–Stout. She uses her prior teaching experience at the middle school, high school, and university levels to facilitate university instructors' professional development. She currently serves on the University of Wisconsin System—Office of Professional and Instructional Development's (OPID) advisory council. Her research interests focus on effective professional development models in higher education and high impact practices.

Kara Loy is Dean of University Credit, Sciences, Health & Human Services at Coast Mountain College. Her career has evolved from rich foundations in the humanities and liberal arts to more recent academic and professional development in education. She researches how professors are leading change in Canadian higher education.

Open Access This chapter is licensed under the terms of the Creative Commons Attribution 4.0 International License (http://creativecommons.org/licenses/by/4.0/), which permits use, sharing, adaptation, distribution and reproduction in any medium or format, as long as you give appropriate credit to the original author(s) and the source, provide a link to the Creative Commons license and indicate if changes were made.

The images or other third party material in this chapter are included in the chapter's Creative Commons license, unless indicated otherwise in a credit line to the material. If material is not included in the chapter's Creative Commons license and your intended use is not permitted by statutory regulation or exceeds the permitted use, you will need to obtain permission directly from the copyright holder.

Part II
Preservice Teachers' Research Thinking

Chapter 6
Preservice Teachers' Use of Social Media for the Development of Their Research Skills

Raissa Mataniari, Asni Johari, Muhammad Rusdi, Bambang Hariyadi, and Finn Kristen Matthiesen

Abstract This chapter explores the facilitation of preservice teachers' (PSTs') research thinking through the use of social media for designing their future lessons. In this study of 64 undergraduate PSTs in a second-year biology unit, the PSTs identified, reported and researched plants using Instagram. In the unit, the Research Skill Development (RSD) framework was integrated with social media-based learning in order to guide PSTs into research skills-rich activities, to frame assessment and feedback and to evaluate the impact of social media-based learning on the PSTs. This research aimed to develop PSTs' research skills through the use of Instagram and determine the effectiveness of the approach. This chapter promotes digital learning strategies for interactive learning through widely used online platforms. Outcomes of the study suggest potential for PSTs, as future curriculum designers, to innovate with social media-based interactive instructional design models that enable improvements in their teaching-oriented research skills.

Keywords Research skills · Social media · Instagram · Pre-service teacher · Research skill development · Instructional design model

6.1 Background

School teachers require the knowledge, skills and attitudes for innovative learning design and implementation that both enable and model school students' knowledge, skills and attitudes for study and work in the twenty-first Century. Instructional designs need to create student-centred, contemporary learning environments in which teachers are developing skills to nurture school students to actively learn, so that

R. Mataniari (✉) · A. Johari · M. Rusdi · B. Hariyadi
Universitas Jambi, Jambi, Indonesia
e-mail: raissamataniari@unja.ac.id

F. K. Matthiesen
University of Göttingen, Göttingen, Germany

students are able to excel in their future career. In such Science teaching contexts, these skills may be thought of as parallel to the dynamic processes involved in research thinking.

A variety of Social media platforms are potentially effective for integration with learning activities that facilitate the development of research thinking, including Google docs, Twiki, Twitter, Wiki, Social Networking Sites (SNS), Scholar Messaging, Instagram, and Blogs. Therefore, social media integration in learning activities has been promoted for its active student engagement resulting in improved learning outcomes around research thinking (Brescia & Miller, 2006). For example, previous research on the use of social media in learning, found Blogs to be effective reflective devices (Brescia & Miller, 2006; Ferdig & Trammell, 2004), social networking sites were found to improve cognitive skills (Akbari et al., 2015), Interpersonal applications and sites enhanced problem solving skills (Zainuddin et al., 2017), and the use of forums enhanced communication skills (Liu et al., 2013). The learning theories that contribute to our understanding of research thinking developed though social media and the relevance of collective learning to social media use in education are explained below.

6.1.1 Basic Learning Theory on Social Media

There are five particularly salient theories that provide a deep understanding of the interconnected digital learning elements involved in social media-based learning. The first theory is Social constructivist theory (Vygotsky, 1978), which emphasises knowledge acquisition through social interaction and experience. Vygotsky also introduced the term 'learning zone', which consists of the zone of actual development and zone of proximal development, where the two zones are connected by social interaction and experience (Vygotsky, 1978). From this theoretical perspective, diverse educational and developmental background of individual students could be effectively brought together for mutually-informed learning by technology-based online platforms.

Second, social cognitive theory suggests an association between learning elements. Social cognitive theory (Bandura, 1986) posits that knowledge acquisition happens through modelling and observing processes. Within these two processes, three learning elements, human, environment and behaviour, need to be associated with each other (Bandura, 1986). The association may be potentially more effective when facilitated with technology.

Third, social connectivism theory proposes six characteristics of knowledge including knowledge that: (i) requires multiple opinions, (ii) requires relationship between information, (iii) may be stored by computers, (iv) requires connection, (v) should be up to date, (vi) is used for decision making (Siemens, 2005). From this standpoint, social media might be essential due to its features in harmonizing individuals' diverse personal knowledge. This perspective associates with the features provided by social media, such as user-generated content, content sharing, and community formation.

Fourth, multimedia learning cognitive theory that elaborates on the knowledge acquisition process. Multimedia learning cognitive theory (Mayer, 2005) explains how knowledge could be considered more interesting if delivered through social media, visualization and text, which is then processed through the sensory system, working memory or long-term memory.

Fifth, social interaction theory, which is divided into social information process theory, situated learning theory and collaborative learning theory supported by computers. Social information process theory (Walther, 1992, 1996; Walther & Burgoon, 1992) emphasizes the mandatory existence of concrete communication from educators, when the delivered communication to the students is considered to be insufficient.

In addition, situated learning theory (Lave & Wenger, 1991) recommends social interaction in the learning process which is later able to be used in communities, as a massive support for the knowledge acquisition process. Social interaction (Koschmann, 1996) also encompasses collaborative learning theory which emphasizes the collaboration element in learning without limitation of space and time.

In this research all the above theories provide a consistent message emphasising social environment in the context of self-directed social media-based learning. Taken together, the overarching emphasis of all these theories is a student self-directed-but-social dynamic, best developed in interactive, highly engaged learning contexts. Applying that emphasis to this current study, research thinking is best developed in highly interactive, collective learning. This study's use of social media in the science education context platforms both require and enable Preservice Teacher (PST) research thinking.

6.1.2 Collective Learning and Social Media

Despite the above theoretical advantages, group learning with collaboration often encounters challenges related to the amount of time required for activities. Building on and consolidating the above theories, Collective Learning is the idea that learning within a group is the most effective and efficient form of learning (Agarwal, 2011). Collective Learning is a learning-based instruction model where students are empowered to explore, experience, and teach themselves new technologies independently (Agarwal, 2011).

Features of social media that support meaningful learning include ease of use and access, permanent, global, instant communication, and simplicity of use (Agarwal, 2011). Boyd (2007) stated that social media-based learning is easy to implement due to the fact that it is so close to the existing use of social media and all its features in daily student life. Social media-based learning could answer the challenges of collective learning, which prioritises collaboration, yet otherwise may encounter difficulties due to the time-consuming nature of collaborative activities. Therefore, social media-based instructional design models have the potential to support curriculum implementation by providing dynamic learning environments (Finlayson et al., 2009). Social media-based learning may build student learning motivation through the involvement of educational stakeholders, including the students, in designing the model.

6.2 Context

In order to understand how Social media-based learning can be used to develop research skills, it is important to first appreciate the context for this study, initial teacher education in Indonesia during COVID-19 lockdown. The need for a social media approach and the use of the Research Skill Development (RSD) framework in the unit are explained next.

6.2.1 The Need for Social Media-Based Instructional Design

Learning activities have been evolving into more autonomous forms along with the existence of alternative learning systems. Chu (2020) categorized learning as formal learning (Chu, 2014), informal learning related to daily life (Halliday-Wynes & Beddie, 2019) and mobile learning (Wong & Looi, 2011). Ideally, the three types of learning are integrated in the curriculum. Social media-based learning is in the category of mobile learning. Mobile learning is a self-directed learning (Kukulska-Hulme & Viberg, 2018), using personal gadgets (Chan et al., 2006), and is conducted in an environment that is similar to a social environment, which has the potential to make the learning more meaningful for students.

Social media integration in learning has been explored by researchers in the field of education. Research by Nielsen (2018) suggests that students aged over 18 years old spend more than 45 min per day on social media. Chu (2020) found that the social media sites most effective for learning were: Google docs, Twiki, Twitter, Wiki, Social Networking Sites (SNS), Scholar Messaging, Instagram, and Blogs. The use of social media in learning has been considered to be able to improve collaboration skills, interaction, academic performance, learning effectivity, support, knowledge management and reflection (Akbari et al., 2015; Brescia & Miller, 2006; Ferdig & Trammell, 2004; Liu et al., 2013; Zainuddin et al., 2017), where these skills are akin to the skills associated with research (Willison & O'Regan, 2007) and required by teachers when they are both immediately and strategically responsive.

The existing research on social media integration in learning does not necessarily provide Educators with the guidance that they need such as learning designer principles for social media-based learning. Moreover, there is minimal research on social media-based design models for the higher education context (Mataniari et al., 2020). In order to address the need for social media-based instructional design models, this study probed the integration of social media in a Plant Taxonomy class for PSTs, aiming to nurture their research skills for their future teaching. The RSD framework was used by the Teacher Educators (TE) to inform the design of the social media-based Plant Taxonomy course. The implementation of this action research was expected to give PSTs insight on creating their own social media-based learning for their future careers. Furthermore, the research would address the gap above, by providing deep insights into one social media-based learning design model for the higher education context.

6.2.2 Current Study: The Facilitation of Preservice Teachers' Research Thinking

In this study of undergraduate PSTs in their second year of initial teacher education, the Research Skill Development (RSD) framework was integrated with social media-based learning in order to guide PSTs into activities that richly elicited research skills to frame assessment and feedback. Previously, the RSD framework has shown its effectiveness in improving PSTs' research skill when implemented in social media-based learning using blogs (Mataniari, 2017; Mataniari et al., 2020). Mataniari (2017) and Mataniari et al. (2020) found that PSTs' critical thinking skills through RSD-integrated lab report indicated improvement through blog-based writing activities, where PSTs' research skills evolved when they were guided by RSD framework. Thus, in this research, the RSD framework was applied within social media-based learning. In this project, we determined to see how a focus on each of the RSD framework facets (see Chap. 1 in this book) helped to develop and improve biology education PST research skills in the context of a plant taxonomy course in which *Instagram* was used as the social media platform. *Instagram* was chosen as the social media used in this study due to its popularity among Educators (Carpenter et al., 2020) and its compatible features for Biology learning, since the platform focuses more on photos, videos, interactions and responses compared to other social media platforms (Douglas et al., 2019).

Due to the aim of the study in nurturing PSTs' research skills, research-based learning was enacted by providing the PSTs with research on Plant Taxonomy as their major learning source. One piece of research that was given to the PSTs at the beginning of the course was a study by Rembold et al. (2017) that identified plants found in the Jambi province of Indonesia, in which this study was set.

The role of the six RSD facets in structuring the course to help PSTs' research skill improvement is shown in Fig. 6.1. In the figure, the blue rectangles describe Instagram-based Plant Taxonomy activities and the black circles show the RSD facets involved in every activity.

There are eight main activities that the PSTs are required to do within the one semester Plant Taxonomy course as shown in Fig. 6.1: (1) Initiate activities according to the instruction given by the Educator regarding the social media-based activities

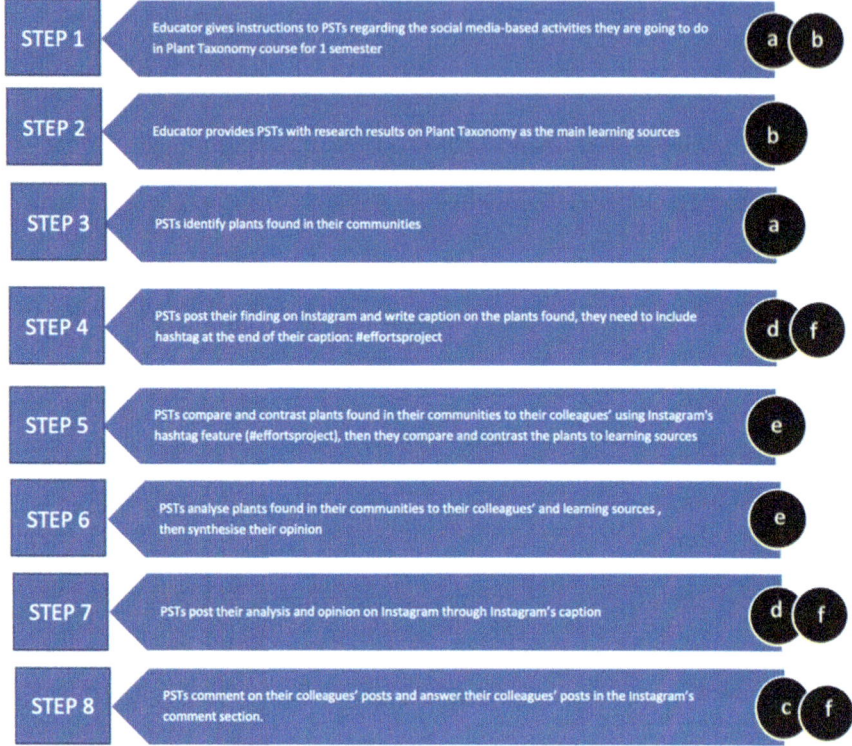

Fig. 6.1 Plant Taxonomy activities with the RSD facets involved: **a** Embark & Clarify (Purposive Thinking); **b** Find & Generate (Informed Thinking); **c** Evaluate & Reflect (Astute Thinking); **d** Organise & Manage (Harmonising Thinking); **e** Analyse & Synthesise (Insightful Thinking); **f** Communicate & Apply (Externalised Thinking)

they are going to do in Plant Taxonomy course, (2) Comprehend the main sources for the social media-based Plant Taxonomy activities, (3) Identify plants found in their communities, (4) Post the findings on Instagram and write captions on the plants found, (5) Compare and contrast plants found in the local communities to colleagues' and learning sources using Instagram's hashtag features, (6) Analyse plants found in their communities and synthesise their opinion, (7) Post the analysis and opinion on Instagram through Instagram's caption, (8) Comment on colleagues' posts and answer colleagues' posts in the Instagram's comment section. The eight activities were designed using the RSD framework to nurture PSTs' research skills and assessed using RSD rubric as shown in Table 6.1.

The first author had been involved in Plant Taxonomy curriculum design before the implementation of this research and was the instructional designer of this social media-based learning unit. A discussion with the coordinators of the course regarding an innovation needed for PSTs in order to achieve a better academic performance and skills in the course instigated the research. The participants in this study were 64

Table 6.1 RSD rubric as the guidelines for PSTs in creating Instagram posts

Item (a–f)	Unsatisfactory (1) Participant would benefit from tighter boundaries and more direction from the educator	Satisfactory (2) Participants work successfully in this open inquiry with structured guidelines	Highly Satisfactory (3) Participants work at a high level in this open inquiry with structured guidelines
a. Embark & Clarify Embark on research and clarify the knowledge that is needed	• The learning goals of Plant Taxonomy Course are not clearly aligned with the Instagram posts	• The learning goals of the Plant Taxonomy Course demonstrate some alignment with the Instagram posts	• The learning goals of the Plant Taxonomy Course are well-aligned with the Instagram posts
b. Find & Generate Find and generate needed information/ data using appropriate methodology	• Information on Plant Taxonomy is included in the Instagram posts, but not becoming the main focus	• Information on Plant Taxonomy is the main focus of the Instagram posts	• Comprehensive information on Plant Taxonomy is the main focus of the Instagram posts and addressed clearly
c. Evaluate & Reflect Evaluate information/ data and reflect on the research processes used	• No comparison and contrast between the given knowledge on Plant Taxonomy and the participant's personal view within the Instagram posts	• Include comparison and contrast between the given knowledge on Plant Taxonomy and the participant's personal view within the Instagram posts	• Include comparison and contrast between the given knowledge on Plant Taxonomy, the participant's personal view and information from other sources within the Instagram posts
d. Organise & Manage Organise information collected/ generated and manage research processes	• The Instagram posts' design is not presented in a structured and coherent way	• The Instagram posts' design is presented in a structured and coherent way	• The Instagram posts' design is presented in a structured and coherent way, creative and easy to follow
e. Analyse & Synthesise Analyse information/ data and synthesise new knowledge to produce coherent understandings	• The Instagram posts' elements are not self-explanatory	• Some of the Instagram posts' elements are self-explanatory	• The overall Instagram posts' elements are self-explanatory

(continued)

Table 6.1 (continued)

Item (a–f)	Unsatisfactory (1) Participant would benefit from tighter boundaries and more direction from the educator	Satisfactory (2) Participants work successfully in this open inquiry with structured guidelines	Highly Satisfactory (3) Participants work at a high level in this open inquiry with structured guidelines
f. Communicate and Apply Write, present and perform the processes, understandings and applications of the research, and respond to feedback, accounting for ethical, social and cultural (ESC) issues	• Language used in the Instagram posts is difficult to understand	• Language used in the Instagram posts is easy to understand, but without any reference	• Language used in the Instagram posts is easy to understand with references

undergraduate PSTs enrolled in a Plant Taxonomy class, in the Faculty of Education at Jambi University, Indonesia.

During the course, the RSD framework was introduced to the PSTs and integrated into the curriculum in order to nurture PSTs' research skills. This research focused in the preparation of future in-service Teachers, thus 64 PSTs participated in this study, they were involved in social media-based learning activity and expected to gain insight on creating their own social media-based learning for their future careers. PSTs' research thinking development through the use of social media was analysed in this research.

By the end of the course, the PSTs involved in the Plant Taxonomy course were expected to critically compare and contrast the plants they found in their community to relevant research on plant identification (Rembold et al., 2017). PSTs also identified the development of their research skills through the learning activities in the course integrated by the RSD framework, with the six facets of RSD set to be the indicators of PSTs' research skills development.

6.3 Methodology

The study was based on an action research approach with an aim to explore the facilitation of PSTs' research thinking through the use of social media while studying in a Plant Taxonomy course with the RSD-integrated curriculum. There were five underlying ideas on the action research use in this project. The five reasons are relevant with the purposes of action research as addressed by Norton (2009). First, as a training for the TEs to systematically analyse their own practice. Second, as an aid to reflective process which leads action. Third, as a method of enhancing PSTs learning experience. Fourth, as a method of improving the quality of teaching and learning in universities. Fifth, as a process which can bridge the theory–practice gap in university learning and teaching.

The action research employed five steps, in keeping with Norton (2009): (1) identifying the issue, (2) thinking ways to tackle it, (3) doing it, (4) evaluating it and (5) modifying future practice. In the first step, educator identified the need to explore the facilitation of PSTs' research thinking through the use of social media for designing their future lessons. In the second step, an implementation was designed to facilitate PSTs' research thinking through the use of social media in Plant Taxonomy course. The third step was when the implementation conducted as elaborated in Fig. 6.1. The fourth step was then carried out through a questionnaire about PST perceptions of social-media implementation and their own social media performance in the Plant Taxonomy Instagram posts. Lastly, the fifth step addressed future practice of social media-based learning, highlighting the need of social media-based instructional design model to facilitate PSTs' research skills, so that in the future they could use the model for their own future teaching. In this action research process, the TEs modelled to the PSTs ways to be both immediately and strategically responsive.

6.3.1 Data Generation

Data sources were PSTs' responses to a questionnaire capturing PSTs' perceptions after one semester implementation and PSTs' social media posts within the Plant Taxonomy social media-based learning through their Plant Taxonomy Instagram posts.

6.3.1.1 Questionnaire

Research participants were given time by the Secretary of Science Department in the final course session to answer the online questionnaire. The questionnaire was fronted by a participant information sheet indicating that participation was voluntary, and that the completion of 14 Likert scale questions indicated PSTs' agreement to participate. The questionnaires were anonymous and captured the PSTs' perceptions of the use of social media for their research skill development (see Table 6.2) In terms of data security, only the researcher had access to the data. The data was de-identified so that PST's individual information would not be identifiable. All the 64 PSTs enrolled in the course agreed to participate in both surveys and Instagram-based activities.

Questionnaire results and PSTs' social media performances were examined. The questionnaire's seven-point Likert scale questions provided data about PSTs attitudes towards the use of the social media-based learning during one semester implementation. On the seven scales used, '7' means 'strongly agree', '4' is neutral and '1'

Table 6.2 PST self-perception questionnaire responses (N = 64)

Question number	Mean	SD	Broad agreement (%)	Items (1 strongly disagree, 4 = neutral 7 is strongly agree)
1	5.13	1.09	69	I am good at research skills in general
2	5.25	1.07	77	I am good at research skills in laboratory activities in plant biology
3	5.69	1.22	86	The Instagram-based activities in this course have helped me to comprehend learning purpose and skills we would be able to nurture
4	6.02	1.29	88	The Instagram-based activities in this course have helped me to gather information and data on Plant Taxonomy
5	5.72	1.27	83	The Instagram-based activities in this course have helped me to generate alternative ideas on Plant Taxonomy
6	5.73	1.25	83	The Instagram-based activities in this course have helped me to manage resources and teams during the Plant Taxonomy laboratory activities
7	6.28	1.06	89	The Instagram-based activities in this course have helped me to analyse, evaluate and reflect the information and data on Plant Taxonomy
8	5.78	1.23	88	The Instagram-based activities in this course have helped me to synthesise the information and data on Plant Taxonomy
9	5.25	1.41	73	The Instagram-based activities in this course have helped me to communicate orally what I understand from Plant Taxonomy lab activities
10	5.83	1.27	81	The Instagram-based activities in this course have helped me to communicate in writing what I understand from Plant Taxonomy lab activities
11	5.98	1.15	91	The ability to research in learning biology will be important in my career

(continued)

Table 6.2 (continued)

Question number	Mean	SD	Broad agreement (%)	Items (1 strongly disagree, 4 = neutral 7 is strongly agree)
12	6.08	1.03	91	Getting involved in social media-based activities will be beneficial for my future career
13	6.22	1.03	91	As future biology teacher, I believe social media-based learning activities will be interesting to be implemented in biology learning
14	5.59	1.28	80	I am interested to further explore research data on plants found in Jambi Province

means 'strongly disagree'. The Likert's scale items in the questionnaire were written specifically to highlight the six RSD facets.

6.3.1.2 Social Media Performance

In addition to the data collection process, PSTs' social media performances within one semester of the social media-based learning implementation were determined through their Plant Taxonomy Instagram post. Table 6.1 shows the RSD rubric as the guidelines for PSTs in creating Instagram posts, purposed to reflect the objectives and goals of the Plant Taxonomy course. The rubric reflecting six RSD facets was adapted from www.rsd.edu.au and validated through Focus Group Discussion conducted with three experts in the field of biology education. The PSTs' Plant Taxonomy Instagram posts were the final project of the course, marked by the educator using the rubric to assess PSTs' social media performance.

6.3.2 *Data Analysis*

Descriptive statistics (mean, standard deviation and broad agreement) were implemented to analyse the PSTs' questionnaires. The data from the social media performance were categorised into the three levels of the RSD rubric And analysed from the perspective of each of the six RSD facets to reveal evidence of student research skills employed.

6.4 Results

The PST self-perception questionnaire showed that Instagram-based activities (Questions 3–14) contributed positively as the students perceived that their specific research skills (Items 3–10) were stronger than their more general research skills (Items 1 and 2), and the former's mean scores varied from the lowest 5.25 (Communicate orally) to the highest 6.28, as shown in Table 6.2.

Figure 6.2 shows a summary of PSTs' Plant Taxonomy Instagram post performance according to the educator who marked against the RSD rubric level (see Table 6.1) for each RSD facet. As can be seen from Fig. 6.2, most of the PSTs achieved the highest level of research skills (Level 3) as a result of one-semester Plant Taxonomy activities as detailed in Fig. 6.1. In other words, according to the assessment of the student products, the Instagram-based learning successfully enhanced PSTs' Plant Taxonomy research skill.

6.4.1 Results for Each Facet

The data sets of student perceptions of their research skills as determined in the Likert scale questionnaire and the faculty assessment of students' research skills are one-dimensional when analysed separately from each other, but the extent to which the data sets corroborate provides more holistic insights into the educative process.

In order to develop PST research thinking for teaching, the use of Instagram for Plant Biology broadly was perceived by the PSTs to have enhanced, in varying

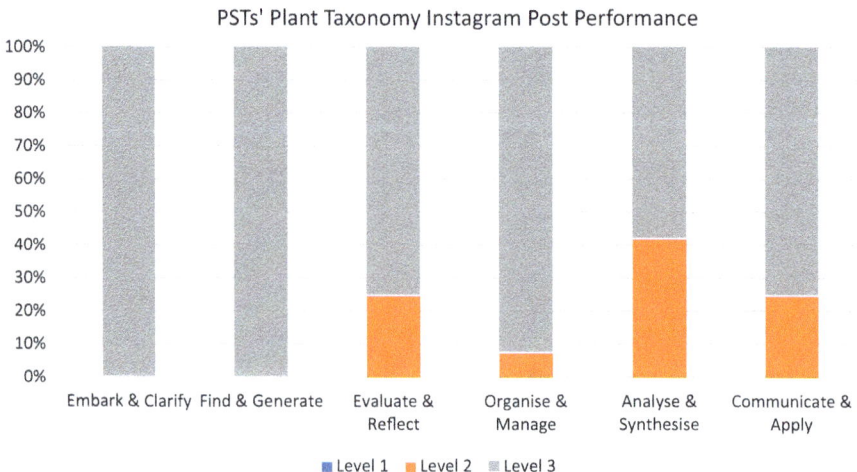

Fig. 6.2 A summary of PSTs' plant taxonomy Instagram post performance according to the RSD rubric level for each RSD facet (N = 64)

degrees, their skills. Corroborating their impression, the Assessor determined that facet by facet a substantial majority of PSTs achieved at level 3 (high autonomy) and the rest attained at least level 2.

6.4.1.1 Embark & Clarify

PSTs were aware of the course's relevance for them as future In-service Biology Teachers to guide their future high school students to notice plants found in their communities and also in Jambi province. The TE of the course emphasized the significance of the course in the introduction meeting in order to build their interest, and at the same time handing the PSTs research-based learning sources on plant identification conducted in their communities.. This is reflected in Table 6.2 which shows that 100% of students were assessed as operating at the highest level of autonomy in the embark and clarify facet. Accordingly 86% of PSTs (Mean 5.6) agreed the activities in the course had helped them to comprehend learning purpose and skills they would be able to nurture.

6.4.1.2 Find & Generate

PSTs found and generated the Instagram contents that they posted using Instagram's hashtag feature, which enabled them both to find and to be found by other content creators interested in Plant Taxonomy field. The activity had been proven as effective to improve PSTs' skills on Find & Generate facet of RSD. All of the PSTs were marked in Fig. 6.2 as operating at the highest level of autonomy on their Find & Generate skills during the course. As shown in Table 6.2, even more (88%) PSTs agreed than for embark and clarify that the activity had helped them to gather information (Mean 6.0) and generate alternative ideas (Mean 5.7) on Plant Taxonomy.

6.4.1.3 Evaluate & Reflect

Instagram posts needed student captions in order to give context for each post. PSTs' activity, when writing the Instagram explanatory caption about the plants found in their community, was a form of reflective practice. PSTs indicated their confidence in their Evaluate & Reflect skills, as seen on their agreement through the survey through Table 6.2 and their performance on the Instagram-based activities during the course as shown in Fig. 6.2. Survey results showed that PSTs gave almost 90% agreement on the use of the activities to have helped them evaluating information and data. Out of 64 PSTs, 48 of them exhibited high level of autonomy during the Instagram-based activity, as assessed by the Assessor, meaning that most of them were able to compare and contrast between the given knowledge on Plant Taxonomy, their personal view and information from other sources within the Instagram posts.

Meanwhile, 16 PSTs fell in the Level 2 of RSD rubric due to limited reference used in their Instagram posts while this facet scored the highest Mean (6.2).

6.4.1.4 Organise & Manage

After the PSTs were given the research-based learning sources, the TE asked them to post on social media a comparison of plants found in their communities and ones found in the published research, which might have supported PSTs' research skills in organizing and managing. 83% of PSTs agreed that the learning activities helped them to organise and manage research-based learning sources when they learned to convert them into Instagram content. As shown in Table 6.2, more than 4 in 5 of the PSTs perceived that the explicit facilitation of organizing and managing data was successfully achieved as one of the core activities within the course. Crucially, PSTs perceptions corroborate the assessor's measures that 92% of PSTs performed at level 3 of the RSD rubric: "The Instagram posts' design is presented in a structured and coherent way, creative and easy to follow by the end of the unit/term", and the other 8% performed at level 2 skills for the 'organise/manage' were enhanced by the courses facilitation of Instagram in plant biology. PSTs perceived their Organise & Manage skills improved (Mean 5.7) and the Assessor determined that most PSTs provided evidence that their skills had indeed substantially improved during the unit.

6.4.1.5 Analyse & Synthesise

PSTs' Instagram posts on Plant Taxonomy included an analysis of how the plants in their community were similar or different to their classmates', then they had to link it to the relevant research on plant taxonomy provided by the TE. It is possible that this explicit requirement was a reason that more than 89% of PSTs agree that it contributed to the development of their research skills in analysing and synthesizing (Mean 5.7). However, the challenging nature activities that required them to analyse information and data might be the reason that 42% of the PSTs fell in the Level 2 of the RSD rubric, while more than half of them effectively analysed and synthesised the results using their own words in keeping with Level 3.

6.4.1.6 Communicate & Apply

The comment section, as one of Instagram's features seemed to support the PSTs in nurturing their skills of communicating and applying knowledge, as more than 80% of the PSTs' agreed that the Instagram-based activities in this course had helped them to communicate in writing what they understand on Plant Taxonomy lab activities. However, less than 75% of them agreed on the use of the activities for their oral communication, with the lowest mean score of 5.2, which might be due to the social media text-based nature of the activities that did not focus on developing oral communication skill. Instead, the Educator made it compulsory for the PSTs to post a comment on each other's Instagram post. Thus, it may be that the PSTs needed to learn how to academically interact within the Instagram's comment section. The research showed PSTs engaged in Plant Taxonomy-related discussion within the comment section, this phenomenon is supported by the PSTs' social media performance that exhibited Level 3 autonomy in terms of the language they used in the posts. Only 16 of the 64 PSTs fell on the Level 2 autonomy for the Communicate & Apply facet of the RSD.

6.5 Discussion

Research skills have been integrated in the curriculum of Indonesian universities for undergraduate degrees, where the students are obligated to conduct a major research project to attain a Bachelor degree. Thus, there is a need for Indonesian Educators in universities to gradually nurture student research skills throughout their undergraduate degree (Mataniari, 2017). This is especially true in the Faculty of Education, where PSTs are expected to master research skills due to the need for research-based learning to be implemented in their future teaching. Mastering these skills addresses the National Graduate Competency Standard of the Republic of Indonesia in which High School Graduates are required to achieve research skills such as creativity, critical thinking and autonomous learning (Pusat Kurikulum dan Pembelajaran, 2022) and thus become responsive teachers.

In this study, PSTs were expected to discern the use of social media for research skill improvement so that they could implement such technology and use the skills in their future teaching career. As producers of research they simultaneously constructed insights in developing instructional model for social media-based learning, framed by the RSD framework. The implementation of the authors' action research empowered PSTs to connect theories and practice in developing social media-based learning, with regards to learning environment, learning theory and student context.

The six RSD facets that PSTs engage in correspond with the six aspects of research thinking as shown in Chap. 1, Table 1.2. The clarity of educator explanation in the beginning of the semester regarding the learning intentions for a lesson, purpose and direction might have supported PSTs' purposive thinking within the course, resulting in PSTs agreement on how they comprehend the learning purpose of the Plant Taxonomy course and skills they would be able to nurture through the learning activities. However, the 14% of students who did not agree or who disagreed that they could independently determine their purpose, and the 12% who likewise disagreed that they could independently find information, despite being assessed at the highest level, warrant further inspection. Some studies indicate that higher performing students can be also more critical of themselves and under-assess their performance (Yan, 2022). For these 2 questions, it is crucial that the assessment from faculty was of high performance.

Student perceptions of evaluation and reflection skill were rated particularly high and yet the assessor placed more students lower in this facet than other facets. The same pattern was observed for analyse and synthesise facet. This discrepancy concurs with research that suggests that poorer performing students may over-assess themselves (Kruger & Dunning, 1999; Yan, 2022). Both of these above finding expose a limitation of the study, in that no observation data was generated to determine, independent of the students or educator, the efficacy of student research skills.

Research-based learning in an online setting has potential to generate meaningful learning due to online features such as image and video collections consist of data that could be used visually. It was expected to attract PSTs' attention and have roles in the context of learning media (Wisker, 2018). The rich features of Instagram (Carpenter et al., 2020) as one of the most commonly used instructional design strategies (Ahmed, 2020) might have supported the PSTs in using appropriate methodologies in choosing, finding and generating the data used for their Plant Taxonomy Instagram post. The way PSTs could look for other students' Plant Taxonomy Instagram Posts using the hashtag feature (Carpenter et al., 2020) might have given them insight about plants found in others' communities.

The concept of student-centred learning requires student participation as partners as the co-constructors of knowledge. Partnership in learning relies upon an environment set by the agreement of students and educational stakeholders in terms of learning priorities, content and direction. Thus, the use of social media in this research supported such partnership, and created freedom (Schon, 1986) through creative construction of research skills without externally imposed boundaries (Willison, 2020) for the PSTs.

PSTs' activity when writing the Instagram caption, explaining the plants found in their community is a form of reflective practice. Reflective practice requires critical self-reflection and evidence-based research to adapt theory to practice, thus it is an important element in developing research skills (Bandaranaike, 2018). Reflective practise also takes place when PSTs answer questions in their Instagram comment section from their colleagues, connecting their findings with research results given to them in the beginning of the course. Reflective practice capability that the PSTs have been simultaneously developing within the Plant Taxonomy course has contributed to shape their insightful and astute thinking (Schon, 1986; Willison, 2020), as shown in their agreement on how the initiative has helped them in doing data analysis, evaluate and reflect.

6.5.1 PSTs as the Future Curriculum Designers

Engaging with RSD framework and social media-based learning appears to have given PSTs insight on how to design such curriculum in their future teaching. Addressing the National Graduate Competency Standard of Republic of Indonesia and the advancement of technology in education give challenge to them to create particular technology-based instructional design model that is able to nurture student research skills. Thus, the use of social media and RSD in learning that they have experienced as PSTs would become valuable experience for them, given that the evidence of RSD use and its effectivity in Indonesian context has been developing (Mataniari, 2017, 2021; Mataniari et al., 2020). In the future, they are expected to make use of the experience to design their own curriculum, as a future educator and curriculum designer (Rusdi, 2018).

Whilst the evidence of effectiveness of integrating social media in learning is well known (Chu, 2014), this study also highlight the use of the RSD framework for instructional design centred on social media. The use of RSD in developing instructional design model includes its use in informing curriculum and assessment design, scaffolding student learning (Hazel et al., 2013; Wilkin, 2014), providing rich curriculum conversations and collaborations within educational stakeholders (Torres & Jansen, 2016; Torres et al., 2012) and setting the assignment task and designing a rubric of assessment criteria (McGowan, 2018). By enhancing the PSTs research thinking with social media and the RSD, their capacity to identify and be responsive to school student needs and contemporary demands is potentially raised. Further research is needed to determine the link between developing PST research thinking and their teaching once they are I-STs (See Chap. 2, this book). This study could be a reference for the PSTs for the design of social media-based learning to nurture student research skill in initial teacher education contexts.

6.6 Conclusion

The facilitation of PSTs' research thinking through the use of social media has aided their research skill development throughout the one-semester action research implementation. PSTs rated highly both on their perceptions about their research skills after the end of the semester and their social media performance as measured by the educator. This experience of enhanced research thinking shows the potential to enable PSTs to consolidate good teaching practice, as well as identify what may need to change, as they connect their university learning to their future career. The research thinking they develop may be the key for them to shift from PSTs to responsive high school teachers who engage with the many day-to-day and contingent learning needs their students will have in High School.

References

Agarwal, N. (2011). Collective learning: An integrated use of social media in learning environment. In *Social media tools and platforms in learning environment* (pp. 37–52). Springer.

Ahmed, M. A. (2020). The efficacy of Instagram on biology undergraduate students in University of Ilorin, Nigeria. *JPBI (Jurnal Pendidikan Biologi Indonesia), 6*(2), 335–340. https://doi.org/10.22219/jpbi.v6i2.12155

Akbari, E., Pilot, A., & Simons, R. J. (2015). Autonomy, competence, and relatedness in foreign language learning through Facebook. *Computers in Human Behavior, 48*, 126–134.

Bandaranaike, S. (2018). From research skill development to work skill development. *Journal of University Teaching & Learning Practice, 15*(4).

Bandura, A. (1986). *Social foundations of thought and action: A social cognitive theory.* Prentice Hall Inc.

Boyd, D. (2007). *Why youth (heart) social network sites: the role of networked publics in teenage social life.* MIT Press.

Brescia, W., & Miller, M. (2006). What's it worth? The perceived benefits of instructional blogging. *Electronic Journal for the Integration of Technology in Education, 5*, 44–52.

Carpenter, J. P., Morrison, S. A., Craft, M., & Lee, M. (2020). How and why are educators using Instagram? *Teaching and Teacher Education, 96.* https://doi.org/10.1016/j.tate.2020.103149

Chan, T. W., Roschelle, J., Hsi, S., Kinshuk Sharples, M., Brown, T., & Patton, C. (2006). One-to-one technology-enhanced learning: An opportunity for global research collaboration. *Research and Practice in Technology Enhanced Learning, 1*(1), 3–29.

Chu, S. K. W. (2014). Examining university students' use of social media for education. In *The 2014 international conference on teaching and learning in higher education: The new generation learners.*

Chu, S. K. W. (2020). *Social media tools in experiential internship learning.* Springer.

Douglas, N. K. M., Scholz, M., Myers, M. A., Rae, S. M., Elmansouri, A., Hall, S., & Border, S. (2019). Reviewing the role of Instagram in education: Can a photo sharing application deliver benefits to medical and dental anatomy education? *Medical Science Educator, 29*(4), 1117–1128. Springer. https://doi.org/10.1007/s40670-019-00767-5

Ferdig, R. E., & Trammell, K. D. (2004). Content delivery in the 'blogosphere'". *The Journal, 31*(7), 12–20.

Finlayson, A., Cameron, D., & Hardy, M. (2009). *Journalism Education as a beta test: Notes on the design and delivery of tertiary 'social media'.*

Halliday-Wynes, S., & Beddie, F. (2019). *Informal learning: At a glance.*

Hazel, S. J., Heberle, N., McEwen, M., & Adams, K. (2013). Team-based learning increases active engagement and enhances development of teamwork and communication skills in a first-year course for veterinary and animal science undergraduates. *Journal of Veterinary Medical Education, 40*(4), 333–341.

Koschmann, T. D. (1996). *Computers, cognition, and work: CSCL, theory and practice of an emerging paradigm.* L. Erlbaum Associates.

Kukulska-Hulme, A., & Viberg, O. (2018). Mobile collaborative language learning: State of the art. *British Journal of Educational Technology, 49*(2), 207–218.

Kruger, J., & Dunning, D. (1999). Unskilled and unaware of it: how difficulties in recognizing one's own incompetence lead to inflated self-assessments. *Journal of Personality and Social Psychology, 77*(6), 1121.

Lave, J., & Wenger, E. (1991). *Situated learning: legitimate peripheral participation.* Cambridge University Press.

Liu, E. Z. F., Cheng, S. S., & Lin, C. H. (2013). The effecta of using online Q&A discussion forums with different characteristics as a learning resource. *The Asia Pacific Education Researcher, 22*(4), 667–675.

Mataniari, R. (2017). Research skill development (RSD)-integrated online report for critical thinking skills. In *International conference on models of engaged learning and teaching (I-MELT).*

Mataniari, R. (2021). *Social media based learning to improve pre-service teachers' research skills.*

Mataniari, R., Willison, J., Hasibuan, M. H. E., Sulistiyo, U., & Dewi, F. (2020). Portraying students' critical thinking skills through research skill development (RSD) framework: A case of a biology course in an Indonesian University. *Journal of Turkish Science Education, 17*(2), 302–314. https://doi.org/10.36681/tused.2020.28

Mayer, R. E. (2005). *The Cambridge handbook of multimedia learning.* Cambridge University Press.

McGowan, U. (2018). Integrated academic: literacy development: Learner-teacher autonomy for MELTing the barriers. *Journal of University Teaching & Learning Practice, 15*(4).

Nielsen. (2018). *Time flies: U.S. adults now spend nearly half a day interacting with media.* www.Nielsen.Com/Us/En/Insights/News/2018/Time-Flies-Us-Adults-Now-Spend-Nearly-Half-a-Day-Interacting-with-Media.Html

Norton, L. S. (2009). *Action research in teaching and learning.* Routledge.

Pusat Kurikulum dan Pembelajaran. (2022). *Standar Kompetensi Lulusan.* Sistem Informasi Kurikulum Nasional.

Rembold, K., Tjitrosoedirdjo, S., Kreft, H., & Tjitrosoedirdjo, S. S. (2017). *Common wayside plants of Jambi Province (Sumatra, Indonesia) Ecological and socioeconomic Functions of tropical lowland rainForest Transformation Systems (Sumatra, Indonesia) Common wayside plants of Jambi Province (Sumatra, Indonesia). Version 2.* https://doi.org/10.3249/webdoc

Rusdi, M. (2018). *Penelitian Desain dan Pengembangan Kependidikan.* Rajawali Pers.

Schon, D. A. (1986). *Educating the reflective practitioner.* Jossey-Bass Inc.

Siemens, G. (2005). Connectivism: A learning theory for the digital age. *International Journal of Instructional Technology & Distance Learning.*

Torres, L., & Jansen, S. (2016). Working from the same page: Collaboratively developing students' research skills across the university. *Council on Undergraduate Research Quarterly, 37*(1), 26–33.

Torres, L., McCann, L., Croy, G., & Mayson, S. (2012). Bridging the divide: Generating dynamic university wide library-faculty connections to enable the explicit development of students' research skills. In *Higher education research and development society of Australasia international conference.*

Vygotsky, L. S. (1978). *Mind and society: The development of higher mental processes.* Harvard University Press.

Walther, J. B. (1992). Interpersonal effects in computer mediated interaction: A relational perspective. *Communication Research, 19*, 52–90.

Walther, J. B. (1996). Computer-mediated communication: Impersonal, interpersonal, and hyperpersonal interaction. *Communication Research, 23*, 3–43.

Walther, J. B., & Burgoon, J. K. (1992). Relational communication in computer-mediated interaction. *Human Communication Research, 19*, 50–88.

Wilkin, C. L. (2014). Enhancing the AIS curriculum: Integration of a research-led, problem-based learning task. *Journal of Accounting Education, 32*(2), 185–199.

Willison, J. (2020). *The models of engaged learning and teaching: Connecting sophisticated learning from early childhood to Ph.D.* Springer.

Willison, J., & O'Regan, K. (2007). Commonly known, commonly not known, totally unknown: a framework for students becoming researchers. *Higher Education Research and Development, 26*(4), 393–409. https://doi.org/10.1080/07294360701658609

Wisker, G. (2018). Frameworks and freedoms: Supervising research learning and the undergraduate dissertation. *Journal of University Teaching & Learning Practice, 15*(4).

Wong, L. H., & Looi, C. K. (2011). What seams do we remove in mobile assisted seamless learning? A critical review of the literature. *Computers & Education, 57*(4), 2364–2381.

Yan, Z. (2022). Student self-assessment as a process for learning. In *Student self-assessment as a process for learning.* Routledge. https://doi.org/10.4324/9781003162605

Zainuddin, Z., Zhang, X., Zhang, Y., Li, X., Tse, S. S. K., Yau, K., & Chu, S. K. W. (2017, June). Exploring the impact of social media on students' internship programs: A comparative study of Facebook and Schoology. In *Center for information technology in education research symposium.*

Raissa Mataniari is a Junior Lecturer in the Biology Education Study Program, Faculty of Teacher Training and Education, Universitas Jambi, Indonesia. Raissa is a Lecturer and

Researcher in the field of Biology Education, with six years' experience in conducting Biology Education Research integrated by Research Skill Development framework.

Asni Johari is a Professor in the Biology Education Study Program, Faculty of Teacher Training and Education, Universitas Jambi, Indonesia. She is a Professor and Researcher in the field of Entomology, with twenty years' experience in conducting research related to Biology Education and Entomology.

Muhammad Rusdi is a Professor, Researcher and Dean at the Faculty of Teacher Training and Education, Universitas Jambi. He is a Professor in the field of Chemistry Education, with twenty years' experience in conducting research related to Chemistry Education and Chemistry and Physics Condensed Matter.

Bambang Hariyadi is a Senior Lecturer and Researcher at the Faculty of Teacher Training and Education, Universitas Jambi. His research focuses is in the field of Biology Education and Botany, with twenty years' experience in conducting research related to Biology Education and Botany.

Finn K. Matthiesen is a Junior Scientist in the Collaborative Research Center 990: Ecological and Socioeconomic Functions of Tropical Lowland Rainforest Transformation Systems (Sumatra, Indonesia) and works in Biology Education at the University of Gottingen. In the field of Science Education and Education for Sustainable Development, he is doing research on interest development in higher and teacher education.

Open Access This chapter is licensed under the terms of the Creative Commons Attribution 4.0 International License (http://creativecommons.org/licenses/by/4.0/), which permits use, sharing, adaptation, distribution and reproduction in any medium or format, as long as you give appropriate credit to the original author(s) and the source, provide a link to the Creative Commons license and indicate if changes were made.

The images or other third party material in this chapter are included in the chapter's Creative Commons license, unless indicated otherwise in a credit line to the material. If material is not included in the chapter's Creative Commons license and your intended use is not permitted by statutory regulation or exceeds the permitted use, you will need to obtain permission directly from the copyright holder.

Chapter 7
Digital Skill Mythology and Understanding in Preservice Teachers

Amber McLeod

Abstract Any assumption that PSTs enter their initial teacher education degrees with skills in digital technologies equal to or exceeding their lecturers, or will be able to teach themselves whatever is needed, leaves all levels of education vulnerable to a mythology of practice. Rather than working from assumptions, this chapter focuses on explicit facilitation of PST digital literacy informed by the Digital Skill Development (DSD) framework, itself based on the facets and levels of autonomy of the Research Skill Development (RSD) framework. This chapter uses the DSD framework as a lens to examine PSTs' understanding of what digital skills encompass. In a dedicated digital technologies unit at Monash University, 190 second year PSTs were encouraged to confront digital skill statistics that question the Digital Native myth, and were surveyed about their own digital competence. Five weeks later, they were asked to explain their understanding of digital skills and after 12 weeks they were surveyed about their digital competence. Findings were used to uncover which digital skill facets PSTs recognised and responded to and which needed more focus in the unit. More broadly, the conclusions will add to our understanding of the implications of explicit digital research skill development for the field of teacher education.

Keywords Digital technologies · Digital natives · Digital competence

7.1 Background

A university education implies more than discipline knowledge. In addition to learning the contextual knowledge and skills of their discipline, university graduates are exposed to new ideas and a wider world view which develops their thinking in a scholarly way. In the teaching profession in Australia, this type of research thinking is known as reflective practice and/or evidence-based teaching and is so

---

A. McLeod (✉)
Monash University, Melbourne, Australia
e-mail: amber.mcleod@monash.edu

valued that teachers must provide evidence of continuous professional development in order to maintain their registration (Australian Institute for Teaching and School Leadership, 2017; Victorian Institute of Teaching, 2022). During their initial teacher education (ITE), therefore, the intention is to ensure that preservice teachers (PSTs) acquire a research mindset that they will carry with them throughout their careers, leading to continual improvements in their teaching approach with each successive cohort of students they teach.

The Research Skill Development (RSD) framework (introduced in Willison, Chap. 1 in this book) includes the Find and Generate facet description "Students find information and generate data/ideas using appropriate methodology" (Willison, 2018, p. 2). The research landscape has been heavily impacted by digitisation, and the skills required to simply "find information" now include digital skills. While some physical books are still available in the Monash University libraries, new purchases are generally eBooks and all journals are accessed online. Data are frequently generated or recorded using digital tools, advances in Artificial Intelligence will lead to "datafication on an unprecedented scale" (Selwyn et al., 2020, p. 2), and the myriad of data analysis programs alone is increasing rapidly. The affective domain for the Find and Generate facet is *"Determined"* and this seems appropriate when the ability to access research, data and analysis tools requires constant reviewing and updating.

In the teaching profession, teachers are now required to have the digital skills to deal with learning management systems, and analyse big data such as Australia's National Assessment Program—Literacy and Numeracy (NAPLAN: ACARA, 2018). From the heart of Australia, the Alice Springs (Mparntwe) Education Declaration says that school students are expected to be "productive and informed users of technology" (Educational Council, 2019, p. 7) which requires teachers to use technologies in the classroom. These increases in political and social pressure require constant responses from teachers. In terms of teacher digital literacy, the most recent demands for responsiveness were associated with the COVID 19 Pandemic (Sanchez-Crizado et al., 2021) and dealing with the proliferation of broad access to AI in schools.

The terminology surrounding digital technologies is diverse and problematic. Simply describing the technology causes problems when terms such as Information Technology (IT), Information and Communication Technology (ICT), and digital technology are used interchangeably. This is not just a problem in the literature, it is a problem across society, and education is not immune. Up until the most recent release of the Australian Curriculum, the curriculum contained a Technologies Learning Area subject called "Digital Technologies" in addition to a more general "ICT General Capability". This caused so much confusion among teachers that it has been replaced with the "Digital Literacy General Capability" (Australian Curriculum, Assessment and Reporting Authority [ACARA], 2022). Further to this, the knowledge and ability required to use technology have been described as literacy, fluency, proficiency, skills, competence, and most recently, agility. Throw in information literacy, AI (Artificial Intelligence) literacy, technological knowledge, media competence and even internet skills and things just get messier. In a recent comparative analysis of twenty-first Century skills frameworks, Bravo et al. (2021) found that "digital literacy" encompasses, among other things, critical and creative thinking, and "cognitive, critical, technical, social, emotional and projective digital skills" (p. 76). Until a clear and stable terminology evolves, the term "digital skill" is used in the DSD framework, reflecting the Research Skill Development framework upon which it was modelled.

In this chapter, the DSD framework (https://www.monash.edu/__data/assets/pdf_file/0010/1652437/DSD-22.05.20.pdf) is introduced to second year PSTs and their understanding of digital skills is viewed through the DSD framework facets to add to our understanding of which facets need to be taught more explicitly.

The increase in complexity and number of digital technologies means the teaching of some knowledge and skills has been sacrificed as breadth overtakes depth. Clear consolidation of the fundamentals required has not occurred, resulting in a lack of coherence in student digital skills. These rapid changes in the range and availability of digital technologies have resulted in assumptions across society that those born more recently somehow have picked up the basic digital skills and knowledge needed without being explicitly taught and that their thinking, their way of learning, is different to those born before them—this is the myth of the digital native.

7.1.1 Double Jeopardy Digital Inequity and the Digital Native Myth

Terms such as "the net generation" (Oblinger, 2003; Tapscott, 1998), "generation media" (Roberts & Foehr, 2008) and most popularly "digital native" (Prensky, 2001) describe children born after digital technologies started becoming common in homes. Prensky (2001) posited that because of their involvement with technology, digital natives had a common way of learning which was different to earlier generations. Numerous studies have dispelled the idea that there is any uniformity in the level of young people's digital skills or that digital competence can be assumed (see for example, Duncan-Howell, 2012; Selwyn, 2009), but the idea persists. The assumptions and expectations surrounding the levels of digital skills of young people have led to unease and inequality. "Double jeopardy digital inequity" (McLay & Reyes, 2019) describes how digital inequity can increase with each generation of students. Directly impacted by the digital native myth, students are able to complete school without learning the digital skills required for an ITE degree, their skills are not improved through their ITE, and once they become teachers, they do not have the ability to teach their own students digital skills. Those who go on to become teacher educators without improving their digital skills further perpetuate the inequity.

The Australian National Assessment Program is used to assess students across the country in a number of subjects (ACARA, 2016). While the report from the most recent measure of ICT literacy has not been released, and the previous one was cancelled due to the global pandemic, the 2018 National Assessment Program (ACARA, 2018) revealed that only 54% of Australian Year 10 students reached the minimum level of ICT literacy. While not all these students will go on to a university education, this goes some way to explaining why PSTs can struggle because they do not have the assumed level of digital skills on entry to university.

Around the world, PSTs are indicating that they do not feel prepared to use technologies in their teaching and ITE programs are trying to address this (see, for example, Lindfors et al., 2021; Kozuh et al, 2021). A set of Teacher Educator Technology Competencies, including knowledge, skills and attitudes, have been developed in the United States in an attempt to improve PST digital skills after a recommendation from the United States Department of Education to halt the downward spiral of digital inequity double jeopardy (Foulger et al., 2017). Studies set in Australian Universities indicated wide variations in competence and confidence with digital technology (Lemon & Garvis, 2016). These findings have led to suggestions that PST should be given the opportunity to improve their digital skills in the first year of their ITE (Albion & Tondeur, 2018). At Monash University only 41% of PSTs rated their digital skills above average, and 12% of first year PSTs rated themselves as having low or very low skills. Disturbingly, approximately a third of the university's PSTs indicated that if they could avoid using digital technologies they would (McLeod & Carabott, 2018).

7.1.2 Teacher Barriers and Research Skills

It has been suggested that the reasons for poor digital skills in education can be described as the barriers to teacher use of technology (Ertmer, 1999). Ertmer (1999) described internal factors, such as lack of confidence with digital technologies, negative beliefs about digital technology in education, and an unwillingness to attend educational technology professional development as second order barriers (Ertmer, 1999). It may be unfashionable to hold negative beliefs about digital technologies in education and, while choosing not to use digital technology may be frowned upon by some, the research indicates that these second order barriers may be justified. While there have been reported successes in improving student learning with technology, these are highly contextual and there is no conclusive evidence that simply adding technology improves learning. A sobering 2015 OECD study showed that across OECD countries, an increase in the number of computers per student corresponded with a decrease in mathematics performance. The report counselled that "the findings must not lead to despair" and suggests that a contributing factor in these results is that we "overestimate the digital skills of both teachers and students" (OECD, 2015, p. 4). Teachers have many things to consider before making informed decisions about the inclusion of technology in their classrooms.

In order to create a coherent argument for or against using technology in the classroom, to determine which technologies work best in their classroom context, or to help identify which of their students' digital skills need improvement, teachers require research thinking of the sort described in Chap. 1 of this book. The DSD framework can be used as a lens for these investigations to determine improvement in teacher understanding and as a conceptual tool for PSTs (Torres et al., 2018).

7.1.3 The DSD Framework

While the university had produced a number of online resources to help students navigate the wide variety of digital technologies in use at Monash University, revision of resources, restructuring of the university, and duplication had created a confused web of resources that students were having trouble finding. It became clear that the university needed a more consistent and encompassing way to address digital skill development. The staff at Monash University library and in the faculties were already using the RSD framework and the cognate Work Skill Development (WSD) framework (Bandaranaike, 2018; Bandaranaike & Willison, 2009, 2018; Revised by Monash University Library, 2019) to develop students' skills, so it seemed pragmatic to use the same guiding parameters and theoretical underpinnings when developing the DSD framework (McLeod & Torres, 2020). Apart from creating awareness of the need for digital skill development among university educators, the main drivers for the framework were to create a common language for educators which could be used in curriculum and assessment, to provide educators with a pedagogically sound approach to explicitly improving students' digital skills, and to provide a reflective tool for students to help them identify skills and gaps. The facets, affective domain, and scope for student autonomy (see Willison, Chap. 1 in this book) closely echo the RSD framework but with a digital focus.

7.2 Vignette

As universities rush to keep up with the latest digital developments, teacher educators are increasingly urged to move away from traditional teaching activities and use "innovative" approaches in their teaching and assessment to keep students engaged and motivated and make the most of data analytics. At Monash University the Monash Education Academy offers online "flexible and interactive learning modules designed to enhance teaching practices" (https://www.monash.edu/learning-teaching/teaching-resources/modules). The modules on offer include "Increasing interactive learning with technology", "Using Moodle data to inform your teaching" and "Using H5P in your teaching" which will "enhance the learning experience for students". Despite the availability of professional development, teacher educators do not always have the digital skills required to develop a well scaffolded, pedagogically sound, digital activity, and frequently assume that if they set a task involving digital technologies PSTs will be able to work out what they need to do. Teacher educators stumble through the tasks and model ineffective practice to the PSTs, who go on to create similar activities for their own students, perpetuating the digital native myth and enabling double jeopardy digital inequity.

The following vignette is included to illustrate the assumptions implicit in many educational activities and the impact this has on a learner's ability to engage with them. It will be used as an example to unpack the DSD framework.

Dale, a PST, is required to create a blog for her first Bachelor of Education assignment. The instructions for the assessment include details about what unit content needs to be included, but the choice of layout and program used to create the blog is up to each student and they are encouraged to be creative. Digital skills are not formally assessed. Dale must send her blog web address to her tutor for assessment.

Dale has never created a blog before and does not know where to begin. She searches for information about making blogs on the internet, but is overwhelmed by the number of hits and clicks on the first link she sees, an advertisement for a paid blog creation website. Dale watches the introductory video and thinks it seems manageable, so she signs up for the free trial.

While Dale is aware that there is a university library, she has only been into the library once and was too embarrassed to ask where the books were—all she could see were computers and desks. She is aware there is a library website with a search page and resources to help students with assignments because her tutor showed it to them in class, but she cannot remember how to access it. She does not want to ask the tutor or any of her classmates for help as she does not want to seem stupid.

Dale struggles through the assignment, using Google to search for references. She is finally happy with the content for the assignment and two days before the assignment is due, she decides to put it onto the blog website. Creating the blog is much harder than she anticipated and Dale starts to panic as the submission time for the assignment draws closer. The blog is not looking the way she wanted it to as there are features she thought she could use that she needs to pay for. Dale is not happy with her assignment, but submits it on time.

Dale receives a pass for the assignment. The feedback from the tutor suggests that her references were inappropriate and she needed to think more carefully about how her work is presented.

7.3 Applying the DSD Framework

The above vignette illustrates the problems created by the digital native myth. Assumptions about the level of digital competence of PSTs made by the teacher educator mean that explicit instruction is not available to those PSTs who do not have well developed digital skills, and although Dale's digital competence is not formally being assessed, it has clearly impacted her grade. Dale assumes that she is the only student struggling and that she will appear stupid if she asks for help.

After grading the assignments, the teacher educator may be aware that some PSTs do not have the expected level of digital skills and wish to improve the task, but pinpointing the areas of difficulty can be problematic. The DSD framework (https://www.monash.edu/__data/assets/pdf_file/0010/1652437/DSD-22.05.20.pdf) provides a clear structure for breaking down the digital skills required for this task and helps teacher educators become more responsive to PSTs needs. It assists in identifying and tackling assumptions and helps to guide the development of scaffolding. The introduction of a common language to describe digital skills in ITE units and the use of more explicit instruction in the curriculum and assessment tasks, provides a model that PSTs can then use with their own students in the future. An analysis such as that in Table 7.1 could highlight areas of misunderstanding and guide the redesign of the task. In Table 7.1 the DSD framework facets and affective domain are included to make the analysis clearer.

As a learner, Dale could use the DSD framework to identify the skills required for the task, and assess which areas she needs to develop if this use were modeled and guided at first. This illustrates the importance of the framework for PSTs. Not only do PSTs need to be aware of the facets of digital skills as learners in order to continually develop their own digital skills, but as future teachers the framework provides a guide to potential assumptions and problems. When designing curriculum and assessment for their own students, PSTs can consider where targeted scaffolding can be applied to help students develop their own digital skills. In addition, using the framework as a research tool to reflect upon student performance, as illustrated in Table 7.1, allows structured analysis and gives teaching teams a common language to discuss potential problems.

7.4 Facilitated Approach for Research Thinking

Digital skills can facilitate the development of research thinking in PSTs. Therefore, in a second year ITE unit at Monash University (the only unit explicitly dedicated to digital technology instruction the PSTs would have in their ITE) the DSD framework was introduced. Unit content focussed on the use of digital technologies in secondary education and comprised of information and activities that were directly related to the DSD framework and the Technologies learning area of the Australian Curriculum. Each week in the tutorials, PSTs were guided in their application of the information in the design of a short learning activity involving technology. Through the successive weekly application of unit content, PSTs had the opportunity to apply, collect, and review data on the most pedagogically effective way of including technology to improve teaching and learning. This approach, it was hoped, would help PSTs improve their understanding and autonomy in all facets of their digital skills In the first four weeks of the unit, PSTs were introduced to the following theoretical and contextual content as outlined in Table 7.2.

Table 7.1 Teacher analysis of vignette assessment using DSD framework

DSD facet	Dale's autonomy
Explore and clarify What is my/our purpose? Determine the purpose for using digital technology taking into account digital practices. (i.e., e-safety, digital wellbeing, digital profile and footprint) *Curious*	Dale has been given a specific prescribed purpose—to create a blog—but no prescribed protocols for how the blog should look. The task asks PST to be at the open-ended level of autonomy and determine their own style for the blog
Select and use What will I/we use? Choose the appropriate digital technology to use for the purpose *Experimental*	If the assignment were at the bounded level of autonomy, the task would have specified a technology to be used for the blog. As Dale has been asked to choose her own technology it is expected that she will be able to experiment with options and find and teach herself to use a suitable program, which is at the open-ended autonomy level
Evaluate and reflect Will this suit my/our purpose and how will I/we know? Critically assess and reflect on the suitability of digital technology and practices in a changing digital environment *Discerning*	The suitability of the blog creator chosen by Dale was never evaluated. There was no requirement in the task to reflect upon the usefulness of the blog or the tool used to create it. As the task did not have prescribed protocols, and Dale only had a vague idea of what she would create, it would have been difficult to evaluate in terms of the suitability for the task. Once again, this task was implicitly set at the open-ended autonomy level
Organise and manage How will I/we plan my approach? Organise and manage processes, self and team function using digital strategies and systems *Harmonising*	The only prescribed guidelines for the task were about the content to be included and that it should be a blog. It was up to Dale to determine how she would organise, customise or manipulate the unfamiliar blog creator, which requires open-ended autonomy
Synthesise and create What can I/we make? Synthesise using digital techniques to create new products, understandings and solutions *Creative*	While Dale is required to create a blog, there are no instructions as to what is expected other than to be creative. This suggests that it is possible that videos, pictures, quizzes, links and so on could have been included in the blog to display student knowledge. This would require the synthesis of a number of different digital technologies that the PST needed to find themselves, putting the autonomy for this task at the open-ended level
Collaborate and communicate How do I/we relate? Collaborate and communicate using digital practices in digital settings accounting for e-protocols, e-safety, digital wellbeing, profile and footprint *Connected*	One of the main purposes of a blog is for collaboration and communication. For this task, Dale has been asked to give her web address to the tutor, but there is no indication that her blog will be shared with other audiences. Sharing with a restricted audience is at the prescribed level, however, the PST has been given no information about e-safety and wellbeing in digital environments and so needs to monitor this themselves, which is at the open-ended level of autonomy

Table 7.2 Outline of Week 1–4 content and DSD framework focus

Week	Content	DSD framework
1	The socio-economic, gender and other cultural factors that have resulted in the gender divide, research challenging the assumptions about young people as digital natives, a definition of digital skills, a video and a quiz introducing the DSD framework	Introduction to the DSD framework Self-assessment of existing digital skills
2	First, second and third order barriers to the integration of technology by teachers, with a particular focus on third order barriers which describe a teacher's lack of confidence in adapting technology use to context	Organise and manage Explore and clarify Select and use
3	eSafety and ethics, with particular regard to acceptable online behaviour	All facets, but particularly communicate and collaborate
4	Assessing the attributes of digital technologies when choosing them for a specific task. Frameworks that can be used to critique the way digital technologies impact learning outcomes	Explore and clarify Select and use Evaluate and reflect Synthesise and create

7.5 Methodology

This research investigated PSTs understanding of digital skills, with reference to the DSD framework, after four weeks of unit instruction. In addition, evidence of a change in self-reported digital skills after participation in the unit was sought.

The research used a pragmatic mixed methods approach, which emphasises joint actions, shared meanings, and the utility of research (Morgan, 2007). After obtaining ethics permission from the Monash University Human Research Ethics Committee, data was collected from PSTs enrolled in the unit at three points in time and 190 PSTs were invited to participate. This comprised firstly of a three question pre- (n = 190) and secondly post-unit (n = 134) questionnaire where PSTs rated their response to statements about their digital skills using a 5-point Likert-type response format ranging from Strongly Disagree to Strongly Agree. The three questions were based on Schmidt et al.'s (2009) Survey of Preservice Teachers' Knowledge of Teaching and Technology. The third point of data was collected at the end of Week 4, after being exposed to the content outlined in Table 7.2, PSTs were asked to define digital skills in their own words (n = 173).

As every Australian teacher is required to have strong digital skills, it was more important to investigate the minimum level of digital competence and confidence among PSTs rather than the average digital skills reported, so descriptive statistics were all that was required to analyse the quantitative data. The Strongly Disagree and Disagree responses were combined, as were the Agree and Strongly Agree responses, in order to give a clear indication of PSTs' self-assessment. Analysis of the qualitative data involved thematic analysis based on the six DSD framework facets. After each response was coded according to the facets, the language used in the responses was closely examined for indications of level of autonomy.

7.6 Results and Discussion

Of the 173 PSTs who provided a definition of digital skills, around 30% (55) addressed only one or two of the facets of digital skills, with typical definitions including simply "the technical skills the teacher needs to know" and "how to use and operate different forms of technology." This fit best with the DSD "Select and Use" facet and resonates with the assertion that simple definitions of research tend to be in the "Find and Generate" facet of the RSD (Willison, Chap. 1 in this book). The DSD facet definition includes choosing appropriate technology, and some PSTs' definitions indicated that digital skills "include picking which technology would be most suitable for your lesson" from "the technology and resources at their disposal." This implies at least a bounded level of autonomy where teachers choose from a range of familiar technology. The affective description for Select and Use is *Experimental,* a sentiment that was absent from many definitions. Confidence with digital technology was mentioned in just over 13% (24) of PSTs definitions. Those with the confidence to experiment with unfamiliar technologies would have reached an open-ended level of autonomy, while those at the unbounded level would manipulate technology based on the relationship between the technological affordances and the purpose and context of the activity. These higher levels of autonomy were hinted at by a few PSTs, with comments such as "knowing how to use and operate a range of technology, including knowledge about the different functions each technology has and how to manipulate it" or that teachers should be able to "maneuver technology, allowing students to benefit from the use of technology during learning." Around 37% (64) of PSTs recognised the importance of keeping up to date with the latest technologies to understand what affordances they potentially offered, something required when responding to changes in order to be aware of potential options. As one PST put it, a teacher's digital skills "mainly describes the mastery of emerging new technologies by educators and the application of these technologies into teaching through continuous trial and exploration." This curiosity suggests the "Explore and Clarify" facet of the DSD framework, at the open ended or even unbounded level, where unfamiliar technologies are explored in order to determine what purpose they could be used for and how suitable they might be for an educational context.

Closely associated with this, and picked up by most of the same 37% of PSTs, was the idea that an important aspect of digital skills was "a teacher's deep understanding of the technology's ability [in order] to assess its pedagogical possibilities … having an open mind to continually learn about new and upcoming technologies." This response ties the need to Explore and Clarify with "Evaluate and Reflect" where teachers critique the value of using the technology for learning. Comments indicated teachers should be able to "distinguish between technologies that will assist or inhibit learning" or "employ critical thought into deciding what technology would be best for each lesson, including the possibility of not using any technology at all."

The "Organise and Manage" facet was recognised in comments from around 15% (26) of PSTs, such as "their capability of preparing for lessons with technologies" or "how to apply it in a work or school environment." These comments are indicative of the practical and pedagogical planning required when introducing digital technology into a classroom and the importance of introducing protocols to organise and manage the students so that the learning outcomes of the lesson are achieved. Approximately 6% (11) of PSTs indicated the importance of teachers' understanding of "e-safety such as the knowledge of using cyber security and passwords." Despite the use of a student Facebook messenger chat group operating in this unit, only one PST specifically mentioned communication, suggesting that digital skills "extend beyond the traditional notion of 'computer literacy' and require a more comprehensive understanding of how technology works to enhance communication and accomplish tasks that would be less achievable without its presence". A few PSTs highlighted the importance of developing digital skills in their own students and suggested that the teacher should be "effectively passing on the ability to their students" which was also coded as "Collaborate and Communicate." They noted that "modelling how to approach the learning process with confidence despite technical difficulties along the way" was a component of a teachers' digital skills.

When educational change is required, such as during the pandemic, a "culture of innovation" is required to sustain changes (Hung et al., 2020, p. 60). This relates quote closely to "Organise and Manage" where design thinking skills help a teacher respond to new circumstances. The inability of teachers to employ design thinking or a lack of disposition to do this has been described as a significant barrier to technology integration (Tsai & Chai, 2012).

Only 12% (22) of PSTs wrote definitions that invoked the "Synthesise and Create" facet. Synthesise and Create refers to employing technology for the creation of new products, understandings and solutions. In their study of 4883 Spanish teachers who taught online during the pandemic, Sánchez-Cruzado et al. (2021) found that the change in methodology of teaching, particularly creating digital content, was an area that teachers struggled to adapt to. As creation of new solutions and understandings is the core aim of the Technologies learning area in the Australian Curriculum, it was disappointing to find that only two PSTs suggested that "this includes being able to apply their knowledge to problem solving." Two other PSTs suggested that digital skills include an "understanding about ways of thinking about, as well as working with technological tools and resources" which referred to unit content on computational, design or systems thinking which are all in the Australian Curriculum and define ways to approach and think about new solutions to problems. Other PSTs wrote definitions that could be interpreted in this facet in terms of technology helping students to create new understandings of subject content. For example: "having sufficient knowledge on technology that allows you to apply it in lessons to assist students in a more effective method of learning."

One theme mentioned by a small number of PSTs in their definitions which was difficult to categorise in terms of the DSD framework was depth of technical knowledge, for example, data transmission, which is in the Australian Curriculum (ACARA, 2022). In the case of data transmission, it could be argued that this is part of the Communicate and Collaborate facet, as e-protocols are mentioned, or perhaps the unbounded level of autonomy of Explore and Clarify where teachers can anticipate protocols that might be required. However, other areas of technical knowledge may need to be individually assessed. This is perhaps a weakness of the DSD framework.

No PSTs wrote a definition that included all facets of the DSD framework. These findings indicate that almost a third of the PSTs only understood digital skills in terms of the Select and Use facet. Of the remaining PSTs, many saw the importance of Explore and Clarify in order to keep abreast of the newest developments which have potential to improve student learning, and Evaluate and Reflect in order to refine their practice for the benefit of learners—an essential research skill for teachers. Smaller numbers of students considered the Synthesise and Create or Collaborate and Communicate components of teachers' digital skills highlighting an area that may require more attention in future iterations of the unit.

7.6.1 Evidence of a Change in Self-reported Digital Skills

The results of the pre- and post-survey in which PSTs self-reported their digital skills are set out in Table 7.3. The initial survey results indicate that 19% of PSTs did not agree that they could learn technology easily and 26% did not agree that they could solve their own technological problems. This does not meet the university's expectation that all PSTs have the level of competence required when encountering a new learning management system or other university websites (McLeod & Carabott, 2018). In addition, in order to meet the Australian Professional Standards for Teachers (AITSL, 2017) and register as a teacher in Australia, PSTs need to meet the digital technologies expectations (VIT, 2022). While it could be argued that the *average* PST has the high level of digital skills required, the university has allowed PSTs with lower than expected digital skills entry into an ITE and they may go on to become teachers responsible for teaching digital skills to their own students.

Table 7.3 Results of the pre- and post-survey of digital skills

Statement	Survey	% Disagree[a]	% Neither agree or disagree	% Agree
1. I can learn technology easily	Initial (n = 190)	4	15	80
	Final (n = 134)	2	10	88
2. I know about a lot of different technologies	Initial	36	33	31
	Final	6	21	73
3. I know how to solve my own technical problems	Initial	7	19	74
	Final	2	8	90

[a]Percentages have been rounded, meaning that they may not add up to 100%

After participation in the unit, there was a slight improvement in PSTs self-assessment of whether they can learn technology easily. There was a larger improvement in the percentage of PSTs who agreed that they knew how to solve their own technical problems. However, there were still a small percentage of students who disagreed with Statements 1 and 3 after participation in the unit.

The initial response to Statement 2 indicates that the responses to Statements 1 and 3 need to be qualified. Only 31% of PSTs agreed that they knew about a lot of different technologies. If, for example, PSTs have only used their smart phone and a laptop, then their self-evaluation for Statements 1 and 3 is based on narrow experiences. Happily, there was a significant improvement in PSTs self-evaluation that they knew about a lot of different technologies without a corresponding drop in the responses for Statements 1 and 3. Overall these results indicate that while PSTs did not find learning technology much easier after participation in the unit, they were exposed to a number of new technologies, and there was an improvement in their confidence to solve their own technical problems.

7.7 Conclusion

To address the continual, rapid advances in digital technologies and the social and political expectation that they will be included in education, teachers need well developed digital research skills because they need to be "responsive to various emergent, contextual issues that both affect and are affected by the overall system of activity in the classroom" (Kopcha et al., 2020, p. 734). This is an important part of reflective practice and in a world where information is updated every minute, skills are often more important than knowledge.

The prime focus of this chapter was to investigate PSTs characterisation of digital skills, with reference to the DSD framework, after four weeks of unit instruction. The results contribute in both a practical and theoretical way to our understanding of digital skills in the teaching profession. The implication of 30% of PSTs seeing digital skills only as "using" technology at a bounded level is that more explicit emphasis on the different facets of digital skills is required. An emerging understanding of the facets, however, could be seen in the responses from the other 70% of students, and while no students included all facets of the DSD framework in their definitions, it was clear that there was an understanding that exploring new technology and evaluating the use of technology was an important aspect of teaching with technologies. The relatively few student comments that included aspects of the Synthesise and Create facet indicated that many students did not understand the central theme of the Australian Curriculum, and this aspect needs to be emphasised in the next iteration of the unit.

The secondary focus of the chapter was evidence of a change in self-reported digital skills after participation in the unit. The biggest change was in terms of PSTs exposure to a range of different technologies, a clear strength of the unit. However, as all Australian teachers require digital skills, even the small percentage of PSTs completing this sole digital technologies unit in their ITE reporting they cannot solve their own technical problems is a concern.

In terms of the theoretical understanding of digital skills, this research has added clarity to the DSD facet definitions in the teaching context. It has also highlighted aspects of digital skills that are important for teachers, but are not clearly captured in the framework, such as technical knowledge.

Many PSTs lack the level of digital literacy that universities assume. This has been a well-established (although perhaps not so well known) fact for some time. The myth of digital natives has been persistent and—so far—resistant to remedy and has led to double jeopardy digital inequity. Recognising that a lack of digital skills is a barrier to the development of research thinking and responsive teaching, it is past time to discard understandable but problematic assumptions and rethink our approach to the teaching of digital technologies in ITE. The results support the notion that raising awareness of digital skills in PSTs through the explicit introduction of a common language and framework such as the DSD framework is a fruitful way to activate their research thinking.

References

Australian Curriculum, Assessment and Reporting Authority [ACARA]. (2016). *National assessment program.* https://www.nap.edu.au/

Australian Curriculum, Assessment and Reporting Authority [ACARA]. (2018). *2017 NAP sample assessment ICT literacy years 6 and 10.* https://www.nap.edu.au/docs/default-source/default-document-library/2017napictlreport_final.pdf?sfvrsn=2

Australian Curriculum, Assessment and Reporting Authority [ACARA]. (2022). *The Australian curriculum version 9.0.* https://v9.australiancurriculum.edu.au/

Australian Institute for teaching and School Leadership [AITSL]. (2017). National professional standards for teachers: All career stages. https://www.aitsl.edu.au/standards

Albion, P. R., & Tondeur, J. (2018). Section introduction: Professional learning and development of teachers. In J. Voogt, G. Knezek, R. Christensen, & KW Lai (Eds.), *Second Handbook of Information Technology in Primary and Secondary Education,* (pp. 381–396). Springer International Handbooks of Education. https://doi.org/10.1007/978-3-319-53803-7_99-2

Bandaranaike, S. (2018). From research skill development to work skill development. *Journal of University Teaching & Learning Practice, 15*(4), 7.

Bandaranaike, S., & Willison, J. (2009, 2018). Rev. ed. Monash University Library, 2019. The work skill development framework. https://www.monash.edu/__data/assets/pdf_file/0005/1719401/WorkSkillsDevt-2019.pdf

Bravo, M. C. M., Chalezquer, C. S., & Serrano-Puche, J. (2021). Meta-framework of digital literacy: A comparative analysis of 21st-century skills frameworks. *Revista Latina de Comunicación Social, 79,* 76–109.

Duncan-Howell, J. (2012). Digital mismatch: Expectations and realities of digital competency amongst pre-service education students. *Australasian Journal of Educational Technology, 28*(5). https://doi.org/10.14742/ajet.819

Education Council. (2019). *Alice Springs (Mparntwe) education declaration.* https://www.education.gov.au/alice-springs-mparntwe-education-declaration

Ertmer, P. A. (1999). Addressing first- and second-order barriers to change: Strategies for technology integration. *Educational Technology Research and Development, 47*(4), 47–61.

Foulger, T. S., Graziano, K. J., Schmidt-Crawford, D., & Slykhuis, D. A. (2017). Teacher educator technology competencies. *Journal of Technology and Teacher Education, 25*(4), 413–448.

Hung, D., Huang, D. J., & Tan, C. (2020). Leadership in times of pandemics: Reflections from Singapore.

Kopcha, T. J., Neumann, K. L., Ottenbreit-Leftwich, A., & Pitman, E. (2020). Process over product: The next evolution of our quest for technology integration. *Educational Technology Research and Development, 68*, 729–749.

Kozuh, A., Maksimovic, J., & Osmanovic, J. (2021). Fourth industrial revolution and digital competences of teachers. *World Journal on Educational Technology: Current Issues, 13*(2), 160–177.

Lemon, N., & Garvis, S. (2016). Pre-service teacher self-efficacy in digital technology. *Teachers and Teaching, 22*(3), 387–408. https://doi.org/10.1080/13540602.2015.1058594

Lindfors, M., Pettersson, F., & Olofsson, A. D. (2021). Conditions for professional digital competence: The teacher educators' view. *Education Inquiry, 12*(4), 390–409.

McLay, K. F., & Reyes, V. C. (2019). Identity and digital equity: Reflections on a university educational technology course. *Australasian Journal of Educational Technology, 35*(6), 15–29.

McLeod, A., & Carabott, K. (2018, June). Who's Teaching the Teachers? In *Open Conference on Computers in Education* (pp. 91–100). Springer, Cham. https://doi.org/10.1007/978-3-030-23513-0_9

McLeod, A., & Torres, L. (2020, April). Enhancing first year university students' digital skills with the Digital Skill Development (DSD) framework. In *Society for information technology & teacher education international conference* (pp. 373–379). Association for the Advancement of Computing in Education (AACE).

Morgan, D. L. (2007). Paradigms lost and pragmatism regained methodological implications of combining qualitative and quantitative methods. *Journal of Mixed Methods Research, 1*(1), 48–76.

Oblinger, D. (2003). Boomers, Gen-Xers & Millennials. Understanding the new students. *EDUCAUSE Review, 38*(4), 37–47. http://www.educause.edu/ir/library/pdf/ERM0342.pdf

Organisation for Economic Co-operation and Development [OECD] (2015). *Students, computers and learning: Making the connection*. PISA, OECD Publishing. https://doi.org/10.1787/9789264239555-en

Prensky, M. (2001). Digital natives, digital immigrants. *On the Horizon 9*, 1–6. https://doi.org/10.1108/10748120110424816

Roberts, D. F., & Foehr, U. G. (2008). Trends in media use. *The future of children*, 11–37. https://doi.org/10.1353/foc.0.0000

Sánchez-Cruzado, C., Santiago Campión, R., & Sánchez-Compaña, M. T. (2021). Teacher digital literacy: The indisputable challenge after COVID-19. *Sustainability, 13*(4), 1858.

Schmidt, D. A., Baran, E., Thompson, A. D., Koehler, M. J., Mishra, P., & Shin, T. (2009). Survey of preservice teachers' knowledge of teaching and technology. *Récupéré le, 2*.

Selwyn, N. (2009, July). The digital native–myth and reality. In *Aslib proceedings*. Emerald Group Publishing Limited.

Selwyn, N., Hillman, T., Eynon, R., Ferreira, G., Knox, J., Macgilchrist, F., & Sancho-Gil, J. M. (2020). What's next for Ed-Tech? Critical hopes and concerns for the 2020s. *Learning, Media and Technology, 45*(1), 1–6.

Tapscott, D. (1998). *Growing up Digital: The Rise of the Net Generation*. McGraw Hill, NewYork.

Torres, L., McLeod, A., Yazbeck, B., Rayner, G., Yates, S., Skrbis, M. Dickson, N., & Fulton, H. (2018). *Digital Skill Development (DSD) framework*. https://www.monash.edu/__data/assets/pdf_file/0010/1652437/DSD-document.pdf

Tsai, C. C., & Chai, C. S. (2012). The "third"-order barrier for technology-integration instruction: Implications for teacher education. *Australasian Journal of Educational Technology, 28*(6).

Victorian Institute of Teaching. (2022). *Annual registration: Maintain my registration*. https://www.vit.vic.edu.au/maintain/annual-registration

Willison, J. (2018). Research skill development spanning higher education: Critiques, curricula and connections. *Journal of University Teaching & Learning Practice, 15*(4), 1.

Amber McLeod is a lecturer and researcher in the Faculty of Education and the Director of Pathway Programs, access and equity. Amber prioritises the development of transferrable skills in young people and her research examines assumptions about digital technologies, cultural understandings of ICT and ways to build preservice teacher digital competence.

Open Access This chapter is licensed under the terms of the Creative Commons Attribution 4.0 International License (http://creativecommons.org/licenses/by/4.0/), which permits use, sharing, adaptation, distribution and reproduction in any medium or format, as long as you give appropriate credit to the original author(s) and the source, provide a link to the Creative Commons license and indicate if changes were made.

The images or other third party material in this chapter are included in the chapter's Creative Commons license, unless indicated otherwise in a credit line to the material. If material is not included in the chapter's Creative Commons license and your intended use is not permitted by statutory regulation or exceeds the permitted use, you will need to obtain permission directly from the copyright holder.

Chapter 8
Undergraduate Research for Preservice Teachers: Navigating Its Rich Complexity and Novel Possibilities

Ruth J. Palmer

Abstract Learners grapple with ways of responding to the uncertainties that currently permeate their academic experiences. In that environment, preservice teachers (PSTs) strive to cultivate complex thinking to master their learning; simultaneously, teacher educators (TEs) wrestle to create instructional designs that facilitate meaningful outcomes. Both groups' success occurs when they adopt frameworks and strategies that enhance the teaching/learning experiences. This chapter reports the results of a qualitative study, which aimed first, to uncover the features of one TE's approach to the design undergirding a research-integrated preclinical secondary education course; and second, to analyze the implementation progression to illuminate those features that facilitated PSTs' engaged learning. The findings uncovered the TE's capacity to anchor the course redesign on elements of the RSD Framework, and PSTs' capacity to persist across learning environments that integrated research thinking into habits of mind routines. These have implications for the responsive and thoughtful adoption of curriculum-based undergraduate research experiences, TEs' role extension into curriculum design, and faculty-student partnership for academic success.

Keywords Undergraduate research · Research thinking · Teacher education · Complexity · Responsive teaching

8.1 Background

Learners grapple with novel ways of thinking, learning, and responding to the rapid change and uncertainty that now frame their lives. In higher education institutions, undergraduate students-learners in initial teacher education programs are expected to cultivate the mindsets associated with novel, complex, and sophisticated thinking and

R. J. Palmer (✉)
The College of New Jersey, Ewing Township, USA
e-mail: palmerRj@tcnj.edu

to exercise them to master their own learning and engage K-12 learners. Simultaneously, teacher educators (TEs) are expected to design and execute learning experiences that facilitate such outcomes. Gardner (2006) defined the cognitive and dispositional capacities or *minds of the future,* needed to navigate these changes. Indeed, when faculty and undergraduate preservice teachers (PSTs) are engaged in research, their shared understanding of Education as a field of great complexity makes clearer their need to navigate pathways that prioritize imagination, risk-taking, complex thinking, innovative ideas, and building arguments related to evidence-based information (Brew & Saunders, 2019), including confidence in their own discovery (Willison, 2020).

8.1.1 Research Thinking and Responsive Teaching

Willison (2018, 2020) advanced a distinctive association between sophisticated thinking—a balanced combination of well-developed lower-order- and higher-order thinking skills—and research thinking. He proposes that r*esearch thinking (RT)* illustrates how **learners** find and synthesize information, generate data following ethical guidelines, and provide solutions to address *issues, problems, or challenges that* perplex and challenge the mind. This brings together dimensions of thinking/doing reflected in other work e.g., strategic planning and its subset, futures thinking (Smart et al., 2021), and Gardner's (2006, 2020) minds of the future (disciplinary, synthesizing, creating, respectful, and ethical). Willison submits further that *research thinking* involves and embraces the cognitive, affective, and relational aspects of thinking associated with a range of students' learning experiences (Chap. 1). This construct extends the faculty's definition and practice of the scholarship of teaching and learning: first, faculty are expected to respond to and invent ways of teaching to capture learners' imagination and second to model that thinking/learning by engaging in research with their students to generate contextually situated information/data and make decisions based on that. In addition, it telegraphs the notion that students working within those parameters can become consumers and producers of research that enables them to make decisions about how to engage in and adapt to challenging issues. In sum, research thinking and responsive teaching advance participation and do not retreat from complexity.

Willison and O'Regan (2007) provided the Researcher Skill Development (RSD) Framework to guide engagement in research thinking. The RSD systematically maps the development of both students' research actions or facets of research thinking and their increasing levels of autonomy. This framework serves as an essential platform on which to build ways of thinking for initial teacher education programs: (a) autonomy, where: students can track their learning by building the capacities for research thinking; and (b) novel instructional design where faculty design robust pedagogical approaches that help PSTs be responsive to their emerging learning needs (Baker, 2022). In fact, instructional design and responsive teaching have recently moved to the fore in Higher Education institutions' focus on teaching and learning with technology (Jaramillo Cherrez, 2021).

8.1.2 Instructional Design, Research Thinking, and Responsive Teaching

Teachers and TEs have been grappling with instructional design and design thinking (DT), especially when no agreed-upon guiding definitions exist. For education research and practice, Razzouk and Shute characterize DT as an "analytic and creative process that engages a person in opportunities to experiment, create and prototype models, gather feedback, and redesign" (p. 330). Instructional designers operationalize design thinking as intentionally planning and organizing learning strategies, processes, materials, and experiences toward defined learning and/or performance outcomes (Svihla, 2018). Further, the American Educational Research Association's Special Interest Group (SIG) in its advocacy for this work has indicated that design thinking is concerned with creating a holistic plan for environments where learning happens, i.e., considering the physical, digital, social, and psychological factors that define the spaces and places where people learn (https://www.aera.net/SIG031/SIG-Design-and-Technology-31). This SIG promotes this field at the organization's annual conferences.

Today, teachers and TEs are reclaiming design and design thinking as part of their practice especially when it facilitates the adoption of innovative approaches like course-integrated research experiences for PSTs. It affords faculty the opportunity to creatively merge design approaches for effective and responsive teaching and strategic thinking and learning, such that together they ensure complex and sophisticated thinking associated with research thinking. Further, when that work is aligned with the dimensions of the RSD Framework, it is anticipated that both TEs and their students can benefit significantly in terms of what Godwin (2020) calls "thriving [together] in an equilibrium of disorder" and complexity. This conceptualization undergirds this chapter.

8.2 Methodology

Thus, this qualitative case study reports on an orientation to initial teacher education grounded in principles of complexity, instructional design, and sustainable pedagogies that inform responsive teaching aligned and incorporated into the construct, research thinking. First, the report describes and analyzes the TE's strategic research thinking design that enabled the integration and delivery of a field-based practicum into the content of a second-year pre-clinical adolescent psychology course. Then, it provides a qualitative content analysis of the redesigned course-integrated research experience, which identified PSTs' capacity to nurture and rehearse the research thinking processes effectively alongside the TE's responsive teaching. The report also provides a descriptive analysis of PSTs products generated during the course as further evidence of their practice of research thinking.

The qualitative case study design with a narrative inquiry approach enables a clearer description of individuals, events, and group settings. It provides evidence of TEs' capacity to adopt research thinking and adaptive roles relative to the complexity of course transformation and varying teaching/learning environments. This approach also offers the advantage of realizing deeper insights into PSTs' complex learning through research thinking and the narratives/stories they tell about their experiences within a changing constellation of peers, faculty, college/school district personnel, and early adolescents in an after-school learning laboratory.

8.2.1 Results: A Focus on Design and Research Thinking for Course Transformation

8.2.1.1 Research Thinking in a Nested System

In course-integrated research experiences, instructional design for teaching and learning, content, context, and research intersect. Faculty adheres to the principles and practice of design (problem-solving, critical thinking, creativity, leadership, collaboration, and communication), while pushing beyond accustomed approaches and pedagogical strategies, to ensure student development of capacities for deep thinking including research thinking (informed, astute, harmonizing, insightful, and externalized). The TE as designer and instructor works at the point of intersecting goals. This section sheds light on faculty/TE's efforts toward ensuring research thinking in a dynamic nested system.

Figure 8.1 presents the faculty-designer's working canvas: a sophomore-level adolescent learning course for preservice secondary teachers representing four major disciplines (English, Mathematics, Sciences, and Social Sciences). This 15-week traditional course required the PSTs as prospective secondary teachers to (1) know, and understand the many facets of adolescent/emerging adult development; (2) become more aware of their professional roles as learners, teachers, scientists, and student advocates; (3) apply this professional self-awareness, to all relationship with adolescents in the teaching/learning environments; and (4) engage in selected signature learning experiences identified by the college, and supported by the School of Education and its departments. In addition, secondary education PSTs are also required to complete fifty (50) hours of field experience, prior to enrolment in the Clinical Practice phases (Years 3 and 4). This practicum was a stand-alone and well-supported experience focusing on Grades 6–12 classroom teaching and learning (Cohen et al., 2013).

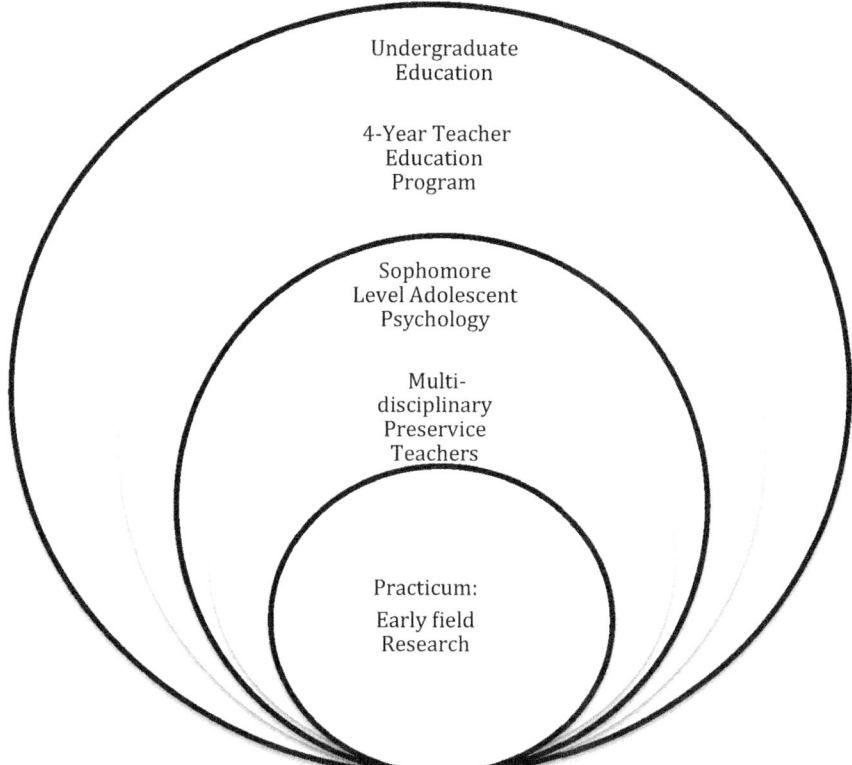

Fig. 8.1 Nested contexts of course integrated research experiences

The teaching–learning–design challenge was to combine these two experiences into one, integrated learning opportunity that also satisfied at least one of the institution's five signature learning experiences: (1) Personalized Collaborative Rigorous Education, (2) Undergraduate Research, Mentored Internships, and Field Experiences, (3) Community-engaged learning, (4) Global Engagement, and (5) Leadership Development. Item 2 was selected. So, to accomplish this integration, the TE collaborated with the faculty librarian, personnel from the Center for Teaching and Learning, the Office of Instructional Technology Services, and K-12 teachers in the school district where PSTs did their field experience. The resulting product included prompts, strategies, and various instructional delivery approaches in which the TE once again became a student of teaching.

All documentation and materials from this course integration, constituted the educator's self-evaluation conducted under the supervision of a HE Instructional teaching coach, appointed by the School of Education leadership. These sources produced a rich seam for mining data on interconnected design, integrated course content, instructional prompts/strategies for TE, layered context, complex research thinking, and PSTs mentored learning.

8.2.1.2 Course-Integrated Research Experiences and Research Thinking

A qualitative content analysis of multiple data sets related to the TE's design of the course-integrated research experiences revealed three elements that ensured the location of research thinking at the center of the teaching experience: facilitative structures, novel integrated instructional approaches including in-class workshops, rehearsal, help-seeking behavior practices, and interactions in small learning communities (by- and across-disciplines). These findings made transparent the threads of research thinking that were incorporated into the TE's instructional design and adoption, and practice of multiple and varying instructional approaches; they provided new possibilities for elevating the practice of undergraduate research instruction and research thinking (Healey & Jenkins, 2018).

Table 8.1 details the elements that served as the foundation of the course transformation: facilitative structures, strategies for engagement including reflection, and rehearsal/iteration within emergent learning communities. While the cross table represents each element as a separate unit, the contents of each section were intertwined to create a fluid yet cohesive learning experience. In addition, it allowed the TE to maintain a creative tension across all activities and helped students to manage both their learning and academic emotions including self-directedness and autonomy.

Facilitative Structure

With the required departmental approvals, revised scheduling accommodated the novel course format: class meetings were scheduled once a week on campus (two sequenced 90-min sessions), and once a week (90 min) practicum, in the after-school learning laboratory in the area middle school: tutoring with students at risk for school failure. This time/activity arrangement distributed class time differently and reoriented PSTs to learning in multiple locations—in campus classrooms, mentored by faculty librarians, individual study, and providing tutoring guidance in the area middle school.

The Board of Education, the school leadership, and classroom teachers approved the tutoring activities. In addition, the syllabus reflected a structured, yet flexible format for in-class and in-lab activities. For in-class learning, each 90-min section contained three movements with a range of active learning approaches/units (whole group small group, individual work e.g., lecturette, workshops, questioning for teaching and learning, conversation, reflection on tutoring activities) with laddered contents. For the Lab, there were also three movements: tutors (a) reviewed together the tutoring goals, including the specifics for that session; (b) engaged with the tutees, and (c) debriefed with the faculty instructor/school counselor prior to departure, and complete the reflective journaling. These routines were maintained strictly for the first five weeks of class and relaxed when PSTs indicated that they understood the

Table 8.1 Cross table: design elements by instruction, course content & embedded research experience

Design elements	200-level course: adolescent psychology	Course-embedded research experience
Facilitative structure		
Revised class structure – Weekly: 2 × 90-min classes scheduled in sequence	Incorporating in-class group reflection on tutoring experiences	Orienting sessions at the beginning and end of session
10 Weekly tutoring sessions 3:00–4:50 p.m.	In-class preparation, reflection with librarian, and director of instruct. design	Faculty and school personnel: supervising
Clear goals, objectives and assessments with variations	✓	Use of RSD ✓
Course/class structure – Units/movements and laddered content	✓	✓
Backwards mapping design	✓	✓
Student disciplinary and multidisciplinary groups	✓	✓
Teaching/learning strategies for engagement		
Active learning – Lecturettes and student present – Workshops – Cross disciplinary conversation – Reflection		Classroom strategies made available during tutoring sessions Supervising faculty and school personnel available as resources
Research-informed pedagogy – transformative pedagogy – sustainable pedagogy	✓	✓ RSD
Creative assignments—narratives, visuals,	✓	✓ A focus on narrative inquiry
Using collaborative technologies		
Reading—texts, research lit **Writing**—Journaling **Thinking** as a Researcher	✓	✓ Use of RSD
Building learning/teaching communities		
Transdisciplinary Collaboration and Partnerships	Faculty, faculty librarian, office of instructional design	Faculty and school personnel: counsellor, teachers, and admin
Building in-class learning communities—shared stories	Reflection oral and written—shared learning experiences	✓ RSD
Students-as-partners	✓	✓
Intentional teaching and modelling of the research process—RSD	✓	✓

new class goals and expectations and established learning relationships with their peers from different disciplines.

Another structural element included the many partnerships established by faculty to support the teaching–learning enterprise: (a) the faculty librarian conducted workshops for the student group/s and individual consultations; (c) faculty relied on the resources of the Center for Teaching and Learning and the School District personnel to provide volunteer training and in-session supervision/advisement for PSTs; and (c) access to tech LMS for students to ensure their individual and collaborative work. Faculty also reminded students of additional campus services e.g., the Writing Laboratory, additional Library services, and contributions from the Student Union. In sum, the TE creatively draws on all campus resources to support PSTs' learning; PSTs grow in awareness of the supportive scaffolding available to help them consolidate their learning experiences individually and collectively.

Teaching/Learning Strategies for Engagement

Reflected in the cross table also is evidence of the extended role of the faculty: to maintain the internal tension to help students return to learning equilibrium-responsive teaching in action:

- the literacies—class readings, writing (class assignments and reflective journaling), and discussions/oral reflection.
- formal/informal assessment.
- Orchestrating student learning (academic) and their capacity to manage academic emotions, whether positive or negative.
- a focus on multiple perspectives.
- TE's extended office hours for informal teaching and mentoring

These connections were deliberate; they facilitated deep/complex and surface thinking that undergirds student academic and affective learning and set the foundation for building the habits of mind related to research thinking. These consistent and interdependent connections when aligned with the facets of the RSD, expanded the parameters of the faculty's own scholarly engagement, into the realm of complex instructional design, responsive teaching, collaboration, and persistent mentoring. Further, mapping, translating, and incorporating the facets of the RSD into the instructional design, nurtured research thinking while setting a path for PSTs to do the same.

Building Learning Communities

Faculty introduced subtly surprising complexity into the learning environment, e.g., by building learning communities, reflecting the social personal dimension of learning. Here, the focus was on manageable, relevant, and purposeful peer engagement, through help-seeking behavior, in-class learning peer groups, and online collaboration, while providing co-curricular support. This approach also impacted PSTs' capacities for alternative perspectives and generative thinking plus a classroom/tutoring culture of collaboration and friendship.

8 Undergraduate Research for Preservice Teachers: Navigating Its Rich ...

In sum, facilitative structures, and instructional approaches including novel learning strategies and efforts towards building learning communities, served to ensure the incorporation of complex research thinking into the TE's course design. These data also suggest that the intentional incorporation of these elements in support of students' learning also forecasts the TE's responsive teaching, thus providing new possibilities for elevating the practice of course-integrated research.

8.2.1.3 Research Thinking in Action: Building Habits of Mind

This section provides a descriptive analysis of the integration of content, and management of the research experience, with PSTs building habits of mind through the introduction of research thinking using the Researcher Skill Development Framework. Here the focus is on the structure and guidance provided by the teacher-educator for students in their multiple learning environments.

Organization and Management of the Research Experience

As a sophomore-level class and the first education course in the Secondary Education Sequence, the PSTs' research was situated at RSD Framework Level 1—Closed Inquiry (See Chap. 1 of this book); this requires a high level of structure and guidance and initial lower levels of student autonomy to ensure understanding and the incorporation of new thinking patterns and sequences. All assignments were then clearly articulated, and prompts were provided for each activity of the research process. Insert 1 provides a portion of the guidance for all students related to the research questions. Given that PSTs represented major disciplines (English, Mathematics, Social Sciences (History), Technology Education, and the Sciences) faculty carefully managed both within-group and across-groups discussion; the goal was to prompt and nurture both disciplinary and interdisciplinary understanding and communications.

Insert 1. The Signature Learning Experience: Guiding Questions

The following questions guide the inquiry:
1. What issues (positive/negative, academic/learning, social/relational, and/or emotional/affective), emerge from an analysis of the weekly journal data set related to tutoring early adolescent students at risk for school failure?
2. What approaches/strategies did you use to address these issues? [*What theories of teaching and learning of adolescents, or recommendations from the tutoring literature did you use to guide your actions/decision making?*] What were the general outcomes of your decisions?

Insert 2 presents the prompts for the journal writing associated with the tutoring sessions; the weekly documentation of the tutoring experience constituted PSTs' data for their narrative inquiry design. Narrative Research/Inquiry helped PTs create meaning from new or different complex experiences that initially triggered disequilibrium, which then change with the practice of the thinking sequence: purposive at first (observing, questioning/searching) then to pattern identification, and making connections guided by astute harmonizing and insightful thinking (Caine &

Clandinin, 2022; Clandinin & Connelly, 2000; Mathieson, 2019). This served to introduce PSTs to narrative research thinking, plus finding meaning in, and having reverence for the stories of teaching and learning, early in their program.

Insert 2. The Weekly Reflective journal: A focus on learner self-awareness and tutor/mentor leadership

The Assignment
At the end of each session of the practicum, compose and submit a reflective journal entry to your Canvas Dropbox. This **250–300-word, single-spaced** entry should include the following:
- **Describe** using facts from the practicum event (who, what, when where, and why) focusing on the needs/successes of the tutee/mentee and on your needs, approaches, and/or successes
- **Indicate** how you as a tutor/mentor are puzzling through your experiences including your decision-making and resolutions of challenges or dilemmas that present themselves
- **Identify** the personal and professional tools, skills, and attributes that you used or may need to meet this or other challenges in tutoring/mentoring
- **Support** your conclusions and strategies with evidence from the text and selected articles on tutoring and mentoring in Canvas Files. Each week read and apply one of the articles

Assessment Rubric: (a) Quality of journal submissions

Prompts were provided for all other assignments accompanied by preparation and assessment rubrics: a limited review of the literature, descriptive data analysis, well-defined report writing, discussion of the findings, and dissemination approaches. In-class workshops aligned with the literacies of focus and research thinking served to introduce and support the assignments.

Table 8.2 places in juxtapositions the learning activities in the practicum, the research thinking associated with those activities, and the corresponding facets of the RSD framework. The internal cohesion of the course, with goals made transparent in the syllabus, the assignments, and the tutoring activities, and the TE's adoption of the closed inquiry approach, PSTs remained connected throughout the re-designed course implementation.

8.2.1.4 Navigating Course-Integrated Research Experiences: A Review of PSTs' Inquiry Products

Engaging Activities, Rehearsals, and Teaching Stories

Twenty-two of the twenty-three PSTs completed the course successfully; that means that they completed each course assignment successfully and were able to consolidate those assignments into a final coherent research project associated with the course content—Adolescent Learning.

When the descriptive analysis of the quality and characteristics of PSTs' final research product was conducted, common themes emerged. First, it became evident from the data that for all students, the first assignments were the most challenging, e.g., reading academic literature—purposive, informed, harmonizing thinking, and

Table 8.2 Research action, research thinking & RSD framework

1 Practicum FOCI: Tutoring The research process	2 Research thinking—cognitive, affective and social	3 RSD framework level 1 and level of student autonomy
Situated within and across class 5 modules	Readiness for the learning experience—tutoring	Structure: (1) Readiness & Rehearsal
Tutoring in an After-school Laboratory	Narrative Inquiry—narrative thinking, stories about learning	RSD aligned with the Science of Development *Embark and clarify* *Communicate and Apply* *Evaluate and Reflect*
Self as volunteer in School District: **School District Training for Volunteers (HIB and Policies for conduct of volunteers)**	Identity: student and learner and student as tutor/leader and learner **In-class training for one-on-one Tutoring**	Developing agency and autonomy *Embark and Clarify* *Organize and manage*
Weekly reflective journal as data collection (250–300 words) Prompts and **Assessment Rubrics**	Identity: Self as author of narrative experience Self as leader, tutor and learner,	*Find and generate*: Types of data Intro to qualitative data *Evaluate and reflect*
Sessions with Faculty, Faculty Librarian, and Writing Center as part of a class requirement. – Intro to research section – Review of the literature	Help-seeking behaviors 1: institutional expertise—Iterative processes Experience of learning communities	*Find/generate* *Analyze and synthesize* *Organize and manage*
In-class workshops: Research methods, report writing, in-class dissemination	Self as capable learner	
Reading/writing/thinking as a scientist: Research literature Articles re-course and tutoring Prompts and rubrics	Help-seeking behavior 2: Peer collaboration Iterative processes with rehearsals	*Evaluate and reflect* *Communicate and apply*
	Narrative thinking: Words, graphics, synthesis, concept mapping	*Analyze* and synthesize *Communicate and apply*
Disseminate—in-class, college-wide celebration, and area conference	Synthesizing assignments	*Analyze and synthesize* *Communicate and apply*
	Oral proficiency	*Communicate* with awareness of ethical, social and cultural issues

reflective writing/journaling. TEs' prompt response to PTS' need including re-reading and re-writing, new behaviors for most, eventually became the norm; additional supports introduced into the class sessions including graphic organizers, individual/small group meetings about the content or integrated work, and especially the use of rubrics, provided options and alternatives. In addition, PSTs reported that their enthusiasm for the tutoring practicum in the after-school lab facilitated a positive shift in their work ethic. In sum, the revised course enabled them to embrace repetition/rehearsals, peer exchanges, and rubrics as essential parts of awareness of learning means to develop sophisticated/research thinking, high-performance quality, and habits of mind.

Some PSTs reported that academic writing was their greatest challenge. They also reported that they actively sought out the one-on-one tutoring available at the campus Writing Center and the Library. In addition, with the course's focus on their engagement, and learning outcomes, PSTs became more extensive in their preparation for class, e.g., relying on the research literature, locating, and organizing supplemental materials to support their in-class arguments, and engaging their tutees. This meant that their reflective journals (data sets) became richer in detail born of their improved observation and thinking skills. These indicate that research thinking, when activated, also prompts motivation, mental clarity, and academic emotions e.g., pride and sustained effort.

Related to this was the activation of PSTs' help-seeking behaviors in both the on-campus class and the practicum event. In their conversation with their peers, PST reported that they discovered common issues underlying adolescents' problems e.g., reading for comprehension mattered across all disciplines, that capacities for problem identification and problem-solving are assets for successful learners. This awareness was reflected in their own journal entries and their analysis of qualitative data. Altogether, the introduction of more active learning strategies changed how PSTs functioned: they became more collaborative, prompting increased class participation and volunteer actions. In sum, PSTs recognized each other as resourceful and shared their work including their writing with others for feedback—for many, a new behavior change.

Work Samples

Consequently, the final research projects reflected PSTs' increasing levels of complex skills, a reflective disposition, capacity to synthesize information and seek out meaning, plus strong academic emotions (pride, sense of accomplishment, positive identity, and commitment to the teaching profession and their discipline). It is important to note that this transformed course introduced students to Level 1 of the RSD: faculty-guided, with limited student autonomy. This means that this experience serves as foundational, a platform on which they can build improved learning and more effective research thinking.

Here are some titles of PSTs' research products that suggest PSTs' understanding of themselves, their agency as prospective teachers, the research experience, recognition of research methodology, and a focus on adolescence.

Student 1 (M) A Qualitative Analysis of A Prospective Teacher's Tutoring Experience: A Focus on Early Adolescents

Student 2 (F) A Qualitative Analysis of a Tutoring Experience: Benefits and Challenges for Prospective Teachers and Their Tutees

Student 3 (F) Analysis of A Prospective Teacher's Tutoring Experience: A Narrative Inquiry Project

These titles suggest that PSTs have the capacity to build sophistication and refinement into their work with further practice.

This 15-week course started PSTs on their way to developing habits of mind related to research thinking. Some indicated that although their new role as student researcher/presenter was initially fraught with disequilibrium, they recognized it now as a phase of their learning development, and an opportunity to explore their knowledge of early adolescents. One PST indicated:

> Being allowed the privilege to tutor early adolescents added to my understanding of that developmental group and of the teaching/learning techniques which work best to aid in their learning experience. I was able to see the varying ways in which individual adolescents differ pertaining to how they learn, and I was able to observe and evaluate different methods of tutoring which worked best for my student. The one-on-one relationship I have with [another student] underscored the importance of a social relationship with students, and how I can establish these relationships in the classroom with multiple students. With this experience, I am laying the foundation to become a successful middle/high school teacher (Student 10).

Dissemination of PSTs Products: Pushing Beyond the Classroom

Since dissemination is a critical part of the research process (Eberly & Joshi, 2022), three levels of dissemination were introduced to students:

1. A timed in-class presentation with an Abstract handout: Required for all PSTs.
2. Participation in the **college-wide Celebration of Student Achievement**: Standard Poster presentation; and,
3. Co-presentation at an area conference with Faculty Instructor/teacher educator: limited to 2–3 PSTs, based on the quality of the work, conference acceptance of student performance, funding, and PSTs' availability.

This task introduced PSTs to another dimension of research thinking-externalized thinking and research practice, specifically communications. At every level of dissemination, PSTs demonstrated high academic proficiency, interest in the innovative course design, and pride in their achievements; many indicated that they would join other school/campus learning experiences that help them further that engagement in complex learning through research.

8.3 Discussion

The course transformation of a standard sophomore-level course into a course-integrated undergraduate research experience for PSTs represented a response to the institution's recommended signature experiences for all students, plus the efforts to make undergraduate research available for all students in initial teacher education programs. This qualitative case study of the transformation showed that Design

Thinking (for teaching and learning) when aligned with research-based instruction and framed with the RSD framework, enriches faculty efforts to respond and put in place transformative and sustainable pedagogies. These pedagogies align content, context, characteristics of the learner population, institutional policies, and the demands of professional education. Frerejean et al. (2021) and Jaramillo Cherrez (2021) underscore the importance of designing instruction for complex learning in higher education; their work gives credence to the possibility of building course-integrated research experiences with rigor like stand-alone courses. The results of this study now indicate similar success when this approach is applied to pre-clinical courses in professional schools. Baker (2022) offers ready remedies to address challenges in the transformation process including active learning strategies and other emotional and social supports. These extend Johnson's (2018) work that provides active learning activities for students and faculty in undergraduate neuroscience education. Both works suggest that solidifying active learning classroom structures and establishing learning communities for faculty and students (including faculty librarians, instructional designers, advisors, disciplinary others, personnel from K-12 school districts, and campus centers for tutoring writing) help to facilitate PSTs' learning through research.

Further, the results indicate that comprehensive instructional design for course-integrated research helps PSTs to manage not only the disequilibrium related to navigating the academic environment but also their own personal and professional identity as persistent and capable learners, emerging adults, and confident professionals (Kelly et al., 2019) who are responsive to the shifting demands placed on their teaching. In turn, they can bring the same goals to their students by emphasizing the interrelationship across research thinking, employability skills, and leadership potential, especially in the service of adolescents at risk for school failure.

However, benefits also accrue to faculty: integrating research experience in their scholarly teaching extends their own scholarship broadly, but more specifically it extends and gives credence to the thoughtfulness, spontaneity, and creativity of their practice (Mataniari et al., 2020; Svihla, 2018). TEs can expand their mentoring approaches within the context of an interdisciplinary classroom while attending to rigor and multidimensional thinking in well-choreographed activities (Palmer & Thompson, 2022). The classroom now becomes the laboratory where TEs alongside their PSTs can investigate and learn about complex learning, learners' socioemotional dispositions, and development in periods of disruption (Gao, 2018).

The findings also raised other questions: what structures are needed to sustain PSTs in the practice and enhancements of research thinking? One response would be for groups of departmental faculty to design and implement a laddered sequence of course-integrated research experiences using other already established field experiences. These include (a) Clinical 1 field experience that includes PSTs embedded in school district classrooms with practicing teachers first to observe, design lesson plans and eventually teach their classes and undertake all teaching activities; and (b) Clinical 2, where faculty extend their role and practice as instructional designers, curriculum developers, etc. Jaramillo Cherrez (2021) illustrates how [faculty] instructional designers can build a research network with professionals with diverse research skills, to create partnerships to advance research and evaluation agendas connected to professional development goals.

The results serve as a model for teacher instructional design of effective course-integrated research experiences that can amplify PSTs' opportunities to become aware of and engage in the complexity of new learning environments. Further, this work has the potential to identify evidence-based information regarding PSTs' learning journeys related to new and complex thinking and challenging/learning possibilities. This information can inform the changing work of not only the scholarship of teaching and learning for faculty but also provide PSTs with the capacities to engage cognitively, affectively, and socially, in the rapidly changing learning environment. In sum, this work represents another step in the direction of futures thinking and strategic planning where faculty and students can walk confidently through complexity and dare to create their learning future. The field of instructional design is multifaceted and can well serve the advancement of research thinking for PSTs in initial teacher education programs.

8.4 Conclusion

This chapter offered an orientation to research thinking within the context of course-integrated research experience in a pre-clinical adolescent psychology course in a secondary education initial teacher education program. It aimed to make visible the complexity of that task given the intersection of multiple requirements related to course design, interdisciplinarity, transformative and sustainable pedagogies, institutional policies, and engaged learning. Threading successfully through this complexity is critical in professional schools like Schools of Education, where success is defined in terms of outstanding future teachers who can function efficiently in shifting teaching/learning environments, an uncertain knowledge economy, and a diverse student population.

Building a laddered program sequence of course-integrated research experiences has the potential to generate a universe of novel curricular, co-curricular, and extra-curricular enhancements for classroom learning in initial teacher education programs: brown-bag lunch meetings to learn to read journal articles, and to construct a well-synthesized review of the research literature; invited speakers on special topics, workshops on research methodology, developing alternative works to demonstrate research thinking, e.g. comic strips, picture books, webpages, etc. These have the potential when paired with current and emerging technologies to change how PSTs navigate through the program—as individuals, as teams, or as cohorts. Their creative research thinking facilitates navigation across the continuum from student learners to practitioners to practitioner-scholars with research thinking as their facilitating competency. Overall, one can anticipate a radical research student culture for PSTs in Schools of Education.

References

Baker, J. S. (2022). Headaches and humility: Introducing preservice teachers to undergraduate research. *Northwest Journal of Teacher Education, 17*(2). https://doi.org/10.15760/nwjte.2022.17.2.10

Brew, A., & Saunders, C. (2019). Making sense of research-based learning in teacher education. *Teaching and Teacher Education, 87*. https://doi.org/10.1016/j.tate.2019.102935

Caine, V., & Clandinin, D. J. (2022). *Narrative inquiry: Philosophical roots*. Blumsbury Academics.

Clandinin, D. J., & Connelly, F. M. (2000). *Narrative inquiry stories of experience and narrative inquiry*. Jossey-Bass.

Cohen, E., Hoz, R., & Kaplan, H. (2013). The practicum in preservice teacher education: A review of empirical studies. *Teaching Education*, 1–35.

Eberly, J., & Joshi, A. (2022). Report writing and dissemination. In R. Palmer, & D. Thompson (Eds.), *Conducting undergraduate research in education: A guide for students in teacher education programs*. Routledge.

Frerejean, J., van Merriënboer, J., Kirschner, P., Roex, A., Aertgeerts, B., & Marcellis, M. (2021). Designing instruction for complex learning. In J. K. McDonald, & R. E. West (Eds.), *Design for learning: Principles, processes, and praxis*. EdTech Books. https://edtechbooks.org/id/complexlearning

Gao, C. (2018). Out of the box: Impact of active learning on future student performance. *The Journal of Purdue Undergraduate Research, 8*, Article 38.

Gardner, H. (2006). *Five minds of the future*. Harvard Business School Press.

Gardner, H. (2020). *A synthesizing mind*. The MIT Press.

Godwin, L. (2020). Thriving in an equilibrium of disorder: Mid-career professional classical musicians' diverse artistic activities in music. https://doi.org/10.13140/RG.2.2.21566.10564

Jaramillo Cherrez, N. (2021). Instructional designers leading through research. In J. E. Stefaniak, S. Conklin, B. Oyarzun, & R. M. Reese (Eds.), *A practitioner's guide to instructional design in higher education*. https://edtechbooks.org/id_highered

Johnson, B. R. (2018). Active learning for students and faculty. *Journal of Undergraduate Neuroscience Education: JUNE: A Publication of FUN, Faculty for Undergraduate Neuroscience, 16*(2), E32–E33.

Kelly, A. F., Bell, J., Dicker, R., Garcia, M., Kelly, E., Streich, R., & Mulrooney, H. (2019). Active learning across disciplines: Opportunities to develop employability skills and leadership potential in undergraduate students. A student and staff perspective. *New Directions in the Teaching of Physical Sciences* (Online), *14*(1).

Mataniari, R., Willison, J., Hasibuan, M. H., Sulistiyo, U., & Dewi, F. (2020). Portraying students' critical thinking skills through Research Skill Development (RSD) framework: A case of a biology course in an Indonesian university. *Journal of Turkish Science Education, 17*(2), 302–314.

Mathieson, S. (2019). Integrating research, teaching, and practice in the context of new institutional policies: A social practice approach. *Higher Education, 78*(5), 799–815.

Palmer, R. J., & Thompson, D. L. (Eds.) (2022). *Conducting undergraduate research in Education: A guide for students in teacher education programs*. Routledge.

Smart, J., et al. (2021). Introduction to foresight: Personal, team, and organizational adaptiveness (The Foresight Guide). Foresight University Press.

Svihla, V. (2018). Design thinking and agile design: New trends or Just good designs? In R. E. West (Ed.), *Foundations of learning and instructional design technology: The past, present, and future of learning and instructional design technology*. EdTech Books. https://edtechbooks.org/lidtfoundations/design_thinking_and_agile_design

Willison, J. (2018). Research skill development spanning higher education: Critiques, curricula, and connections. *Journal of University Teaching & Learning Practice, 15*(4), 1.

Willison, J. (2020). *The models of engaged learning and teaching: Connecting sophisticated learning from early childhood to Ph.D.* Springer.

Willison, J., & O'Regan, K. (2007). Commonly known, commonly not known, totally unknown: A framework for students becoming researchers. *Higher Education Research & Development, 26*(4), 393–409.

Ruth J. Palmer is the President of the Council on Undergraduate Research, USA and Emeritus Professor of Educational Psychology with TCNJ's School of Education. Her teaching focused primarily on Adolescent Psychology at the graduate and undergraduate levels and a first-year seminar on the Pedagogy and Politics of the Civil Rights Movement and Freedom Schools. Her research interests include professional identity construction in teacher education, mentored undergraduate research, and academic emotions in teaching and learning.

Open Access This chapter is licensed under the terms of the Creative Commons Attribution 4.0 International License (http://creativecommons.org/licenses/by/4.0/), which permits use, sharing, adaptation, distribution and reproduction in any medium or format, as long as you give appropriate credit to the original author(s) and the source, provide a link to the Creative Commons license and indicate if changes were made.

The images or other third party material in this chapter are included in the chapter's Creative Commons license, unless indicated otherwise in a credit line to the material. If material is not included in the chapter's Creative Commons license and your intended use is not permitted by statutory regulation or exceeds the permitted use, you will need to obtain permission directly from the copyright holder.

Glossary of Terms

Educational Development (ED) Professional development around curriculum, teaching, assessment and learning for University Educators.
Synonyms used in other contexts: Academic development; faculty development.

Initial Teacher Education (ITE) Undergraduate or Master's programs that enable students to become accredited teachers. Bachelor of Teaching and Master's of Teaching are common ITE programs. In many contexts, Master's of Education is not typically an ITE program, but for the further development of practicing teachers, or those with other interests in education, such as policy work or research.
Synonyms used in other contexts: Teacher training, Bachelor of Teaching, Bachelor of Education, Master's of Teaching.

In-service educator General term that includes In-Service Teacher and University Educator.

In-service Teacher (I-ST) A practicing Teacher. In Chaps. 4 and 5, the I-STs are enrolled in Master's in Education to deepen their pedagogical approaches.
Synonyms used in other contexts: Classroom teachers.

Preservice teacher (PST) A university student engaging in an Initial Teacher education course, whether at Bachelor level or Master's level. In this book, the PSTs mentioned are all undergraduate students (Chaps. 6–8).
Synonyms used in other contexts: Initial Teacher Education students.

Research thinking The *research thinking* addressed in this book involves '…the trivial and ordinary as well as the technical and recondite' for preservice and in-service teachers in their classrooms (Dewey, 1910). It solves a '… *problem* to whatever… perplexes and challenges the mind…' (Dewey, 1910). This is a very broad portrayal of research thinking that depicts how teachers determine problems and issues to address, find information or generate data and solutions, whether commonly known to many or previously unknown to all. Like all forms of sophisticated thinking, *research thinking* embraces cognitive, affective and relational realms.

Research thinking includes the thinking associated with action learning, classroom action research, evidence-based decision making, participatory action research, reflective practice, research-based teaching and the scholarship of teaching and learning.

Responsive Teaching The actions and judgements of teachers as they change or consolidate their facilitation of student learning.. Responsive teaching requires thoughtful consideration that identifies and consolidates good practice, but also moves quickly to adjust and change as prompted by immediate needs. Research thinking for responsive teaching involves teachers' dual role as consumers *and* producers of research that enables them to learn to make decisions about how to adapt to emerging issues, sometimes planning proactively, sometimes responding quickly. Whether consolidating or changing, responsive teachers endeavour to connect the components of learning in ways that students can join the dots.

Teacher Educators University Educators who teach into PST or I-ST University programs.

University Educators Those who teach in university programs. Some University Educators who are participants in *Educational Development* teach PSTs and I-STs and are called Teacher Educators. Other University Educators who are participants in *Educational Development* teach non-education courses that PSTs enrol in, such as 'Biology 101', or 'Media 303'.

Synonyms used in other contexts: Academic, Faculty, Lecturer, tutor, supervisor, Higher Education educator.

SPRINGER NATURE

GPSR Compliance

The European Union's (EU) General Product Safety Regulation (GPSR) is a set of rules that requires consumer products to be safe and our obligations to ensure this.

If you have any concerns about our products, you can contact us on ProductSafety@springernature.com

In case Publisher is established outside the EU, the EU authorized representative is:

Springer Nature Customer Service Center GmbH
Europaplatz 3
69115 Heidelberg, Germany

The manufacturer's authorised representative in the EU is Springer Nature Customer Service Centre GmbH, Europaplatz 3, 69115 Heidelberg, Germany. If you have any concerns regarding our products, please contact ProductSafety@springernature.com

Printed and bound by CPI Group (UK) Ltd, Croydon, CR0 4YY

23/03/2026

02076369-0006